*To My Daughters
Deena & Cristina
With Love*

Acknowledgments

Every worthwhile task of my life has been accomplished with the valuable help of many talented individuals — and the writing of this book is no exception.

My deep gratitude to the tens of thousands of youth leaders in churches across America and the world who believed enough in my work over the years to acquire copies of my books, newsletters, cassettes and other materials . . . and to the millions of young people who participated in their youth ministry programs. They have all helped me greatly in the development of my ministry and have enhanced my work.

— Nido Qubein

WHAT WORKS
&
WHAT DOESN'T
IN YOUTH
MINISTRY

NIDO QUBEIN

MERIWETHER PUBLISHING LTD.
COLORADO SPRINGS, COLORADO

Meriwether Publishing Ltd., Publisher
P.O. Box 7710
Colorado Springs, CO 80933

Designer: Michelle Zapel Gallardo
Photographer: Ted Zapel
Executive Editor: Arthur Zapel
Manuscript Editor: Kathy Pijanowski

Youth group members and their leaders photographed for this book
are from the Community Congregational Church of Manitou Springs,
Colorado.

ISBN: 0-916260-40-2
Library of Congress #86-62111
© Copyright MCMLXXXVI Meriwether Publishing Ltd.
Printed in the United States of America
First Edition

TABLE OF CONTENTS

Section I:
The Effective Youth Leader

Section II:
Focus on Relationships

Section III:
Gearing Up for Action

Section I

The Effective Youth Leader

CHAPTER 1

Youth Ministry: A Unique Opportunity

A youth minister sat in his office one day, nursing a good case of the occupational miseries. In recent weeks, he had felt the full impact of Murphy's Law. Murphy is the guy who said, "If anything can go wrong, it will go wrong."

The members of his youth group were upset that he'd had to cut out plans for their fall retreat because of church budget cuts; the church board was complaining that the youth group made too much noise and too big a mess at its regular meeting; and several parents had soundly admonished him that his programs did not contain enough Bible training for their children. Attendance was beginning to sag — and so was he.

He turned to his typewriter and composed the following classified ad to vent his frustrations:

YOUTH MINISTER WANTED

Youth minister wanted for large group of spoiled kids. Must be able to walk on water, create a whole year's program from five posters and two films, and be all things to all people. The person we are looking for should have the patience of Job, the courage of David, the leadership ability of Moses, the faith of Abraham, the tender heart of Jeremiah, the wisdom of Solomon, the administrative ability of Joseph, the pain tolerance of Stephen, the zeal of Paul, the imagination of John, the eloquence of Apollos and the charisma of Peter. Compensation package includes ample supply of criticism, minimal pay and limitless committee meetings. Applicants must be seasoned veterans with minimum experience of 10 years, hold several degrees, but be under 25 years of age. Our last youth minister died from physical and mental exhaustion and lack of understanding. Apply by writing your résumé on the wall.

He slipped the ad into a folder on his desk, pondered whether he should post it on the bulletin board outside his office, and reached for his coat — it was time for another committee meeting.

As he headed down the hall, a loud, excited voice called out to him from behind. It was a voice he thought he should recognize. It sounded like a boy he remembered from the distant past — only now the voice was deeper and more mature.

"Larry," the voice shouted, "wait up a minute!"

The youth minister turned and saw a familiar form — only now it seemed taller and stronger than he had remembered.

"Chuck?" he said, "Is that you?"

"Yeah! It's me!" came the cheerful reply. "What's happened to your hair? . . . Looks like it's thinned out since I last saw you."

"This job will make your hair turn loose, or turn gray — whichever happens first," Larry chuckled. "What are you doing now?"

"I'm on my way to my first pastorate. . . . Just graduated from the seminary."

"Really," replied Larry, trying to forget the memories of a bois-terous, obnoxious and disruptive kid named Chuck.

"Yeah!" Chuck said with a more serious tone, "And I just wanted to stop by and thank you for making it all possible."

"What do you mean?" asked Larry, confused. He'd lost contact with Chuck after his family had moved out of town. The last he'd heard, Chuck had been a pretty mixed-up kid.

"When my family left here a few years ago, my life was a wreck. . . . I got to thinking about all the things you'd said to me. . . . You never put me down. You always told me that God loved me, and that he could use me for his glory. . . . I decided to take your advice, and turned my life over to him."

"T-t-that's great!" Larry responded, rather taken aback by the whole scene.

"Larry," said the distinguished young man, putting his arm around his former youth minister's shoulders, "I don't know where I'd be today if you hadn't been there when I needed you."

The two talked furiously for the next few moments, trying to catch up on years of separation. Finally, Larry glanced at his watch, broke off the conversation, and headed down the long corridor toward the committee meeting — which was already in progress.

Suddenly, he stopped, wheeled around, and headed back to his office. He picked up the folder, took out the ad he'd drawn up, crumpled it, and threw it into the trash can.

When he got to the meeting, 10 minutes late, he was greeted by disapproving looks from the chairman and several committee members. He only smiled and slipped into a chair. He was ready for another go at coping with the pains and frustrations of being a youth worker.

The joys and rewards of working with young people may be few and far between, but when they come, they make enduring all the pains worth it.

Youth Ministry Offers Unique Opportunities

"As the twig is bent, so grows the tree," is an old saying that has been confirmed by a century of psychological study and experience. A loving, competent youth worker occupies a unique position and holds a unique opportunity to help with the shaping of young lives.

The story is told of an old teacher in England who would always greet his class with a deep bow on the first day of each new school term. It was a strange custom, since all the other teachers always stood erect and waited for their students to kneel before them. They thought it only proper that the students should bow to pay honor to their "masters," to affirm that they were under the teachers' control.

"Sir, why do you bow before us?" asked one of his students.

"I am what I shall become — a teacher," replied the old master. "But I do not know what you shall become. One of you might someday be prime minister of England, or perhaps even royalty. I dare not fail to show respect to people who have the potential to become great."

Seeing young people as "potential greats" is not often easy. In fact, it sometimes requires a great deal of imagination. But don't ever forget, that's the way Jesus always saw the people who came to him. He saw a ruddy, wishy-washy and unstable fisherman as a rock on which he could build his church. He saw a vicious persecutor of the church, a zealous and self-righteous Saul, as a potentially great apostle who could write letters that millions of people would one day call "the Scriptures." And he saw a woman named Mary Magdalene, who "had seven devils," but who had the potential to serve him so faithfully that she deserved to be his first contact with a human being after his resurrection.

Because the pains and frustrations of youth work tend to come daily, it is often easier to focus on them and fail to see the opportunities in the youngsters who present themselves to us for ministry.

But there is another dimension to this business of bending twigs. Youth leaders and others who work with young people can contribute to the sense of alienation that a young person feels.

Star Daily became one of England's most celebrated names in crime. At one point, he was described by authorities as the "most feared and hated criminal in this country." In his book, *Love Can Open Prison Doors,* he tells how it all began.

Left alone by the death of his parents, young Star had only a sister to care for him. He was a little slow in school — especially with reading. Somehow, he just couldn't pronounce words correctly.

One day, the teacher called him up to the front of the room and ordered him to read a complicated passage. The boy fidgeted about, cleared his throat, and started to read. Slowly, cautiously, he stumbled through the words, but try as he might, he couldn't pronounce the simplest of words.

The other students began to snicker, as children will. The more they laughed, the more Star stumbled. Looking for comfort, he turned to his sister, who was also in the class, and saw her joining in the laughter.

Finally, when the laughter had turned into an uproar, he turned to the one remaining person who might befriend him in his humiliation. Just as he looked hopefully at her, she buried her face in her handkerchief and also began to snicker.

It was too much for the little fellow! He slammed the book closed, threw it violently, and stormed out of the room. For days and days he ran, further and further away from the jeering mob and the insensitive teacher.

"They may someday hate me, they may even fear me," he said to himself over and over, "but they will never again laugh at me!" By the time he turned 21, he had left a trail of blood and terror halfway across Europe. At age 30, he was the most wanted fugitive in England.

Eventually he was caught and sent to the toughest prison warden in the country to be broken. "Before I'm through with you," the warden told him, "you will either break or die!"

"I might die," said Star Daily, "but I'll never break!"

The story of how he was converted through the love of Christ is one of the most fascinating testimonies you'd ever want to read. But that is not our concern here. The question of how a youngster who had the potential for greatness became such a hardened criminal, is what concerns us.

Had the teacher to whom that little boy looked for aid and comfort been more sensitive to his feelings of rejection and humiliation, it is quite likely she could have helped him write an autobiography of self-fulfillment and usefulness, instead of one that told of murders and robberies.

Your Attitude Shows Through Your Actions

"Should I get involved in youth ministry?" a young lady once asked a veteran of many years' successful work with juvenile delinquents.

"I can't tell you what to do," the youth minister replied, "but I can give you a question to ponder: why do you want to pursue a career in youth work?"

He went on to explain to the woman that only if she is "more concerned with the needs and futures of young people than with building a successful career or finding self-fulfillment," she should probably get involved.

"Likewise," he continued, "any youth worker who realizes one day that he* or she is more concerned about his or her own problems, frustrations or career aspirations than about the concerns of young people should probably get out of youth work that day."

Someone has described the typical teenager as "a skin stretched over an identity crisis." Most teenagers are lost somewhere between childhood and adulthood and are trying desperately to find out who they are. They tend to be self-centered, hypercritical, peer-conscious and erratic. A youth worker cannot realistically expect a great deal of affirmation, encouragement or "stroking" from adolescents. The giving is primarily a one-way street — the youth worker gives affirmation, encouragement and loving strokes to the young people to whom he or she seeks to minister.

---

*Throughout this book, the words *he, him* and *his* are often used to mean also *she, her* and *hers,* to include all people, regardless of sex.

Now, that may sound negative and critical. But it's more along the lines of a realistic appraisal. People who go into youth work with their eyes wide open, expecting to be fulfilled through giving, reap rich rewards of personal satisfaction from helping to shape those twigs into strong and straight trees. Those who enter the field thinking they will be honored and complimented regularly by the youth and others usually reap the disappointment and frustration that comes from the normal relationship with young people.

Do you remember our Lord's experience with the 10 lepers? Here was a group of people living lives of excruciating pain, abject poverty and complete social isolation. Jesus healed the whole lot at one time. Yet only one returned to give thanks. All the others rushed to enjoy the benefits of their new condition. Youth workers who have been around for a while know that one expression of gratitude out of 10 efforts to help is a pretty good batting average.

The Power of Influence

Children and youth are attractive to us precisely because they are growing — they are little, trying to become big.

We think it's cute when a child tries to act big. A little girl all dressed up in her mother's high heels, dress and full make-up can put us in stitches. And we get a big kick out of seeing a little boy dressed up in his father's shoes, slacks and shirt.

Little folks and adolescents mimic the behavior of adults because of the power of influence. When you are knee-high to everybody in a room, and you notice that those big people are the ones with power, you tend to want to become like them. When you are an adolescent and you notice the control, prestige and freedom adults enjoy through driving a car, or living independently, or having their own income, you tend to want to become like them.

In fact, people of all ages are influenced by other people's actions and words. If that were not true, political candidates and businessmen would not spend millions of dollars each year on television commercials which show celebrities endorsing them or their products.

As hard as it may be to realize at times, young people are influenced by everything adults do and say. Youth directors are often shocked to hear a young adult repeat something he heard the youth director say years before. They are shocked because, at the time, the young person seemed totally preoccupied with something else, and gave no indication of either hearing or taking the message seriously.

The choice is never whether to influence the lives of young people around us, but whether we will exert that influence in positive directions.

How to Become a Positive Influence

"I can talk to those kids until I'm blue in the face, and they never hear a word I say," I've heard several youth directors exclaim.

"What you are shouts so loudly I can't hear what you say," is an old adage that readily comes to mind when I hear someone complain about not being able to break through the barriers that the young people in their group have erected.

There's a strange twist to this business of influence: we tend to judge ourselves by our motives and intentions; others tend to judge us by our actions and what we say. Further, the young people we seek to influence tend to judge what they hear us say by what they see us do.

Crashing through these barriers with the good news of the gospel is usually an impossible task. We may feel that we have the answers to the most troublesome questions youth are asking, but unless we can establish an atmosphere of trust and respect, they will keep their questions and we will not be able to give them our answers.

George Washington Carver unlocked the tremendous secrets of the peanut because he loved it enough to probe its deepest mysteries. He once said, "Anything will give up its secrets if you love it enough."

Peanut-sized people will open up their lives to you and receive the positive influence and insights you want to give them — *when you love them enough*. That love must not only be felt, it must be demonstrated in very tangible ways.

10 Keys to Exerting a Positive Influence

Here are some keys to help you unlock those closed minds and hearts that seem to resist all of your efforts to break through with a message of God's love:

   1. Be real! Young people can usually spot a phony from across the room. The faith we claim must be reflected by the way we live out our lives and it must be demonstrated in the ways we treat the young people in our groups.

2. *Act your age!* Give your young people someone to look up to. People who fail to reflect their true age are usually considered social misfits or outright hypocrites. If you are 30, there is no way you can become a peer of a person who is 13. If you respect the maturity and integrity of your age, young people will also respect it. If you try to convince them you are younger than you are, they will probably wonder what else you are lying to them about.

3. *Be loyal!* Young people can be expected to let you down because of their lack of maturity, but they will always look to you for loyalty. Some will test you to see if they can trust you to keep confidential the secrets they share with you. If they find out you can be counted upon to guard their little secrets, they will gradually entrust you with bigger secrets. It takes time.

4. *Be open!* Accepting people exactly as they are can open doors to help them become what they were created to be. *To accept* means *to receive willingly.* It's easy to confuse acceptance of a person with approval of that person's actions. *To approve* means *to deem satisfactory.* It is not necessary to agree with a person's position or to approve of that person's actions in order to accept that person. Total nonjudgemental acceptance is an absolute must if you would open the doors to a person's heart.

5. *Listen actively!* God gave each of us two ears and only one mouth. That means we should listen twice as much as we talk. There's a great deal of difference between the physical response of hearing and the total attention required for active listening. Learn to draw out young people in conversation with such questions as, "How does that make you feel?" Also, learn to look behind the words to spot feelings and meanings that are hidden. Someone has noted that the most loving thing a person can do for another is to aggressively listen.

6. *Be sensitive!* Stay alert for attitudes, subtle expressions of need and hurts that cannot be expressed. Often those who need love demonstrate their need by hostile actions, or by withdrawal. Sensitivity to the feelings of each person in your group is one of the greatest keys for unlocking hearts and minds.

7. **Be responsive!** The natural tendency is for us to be reactive. When a young person "acts up," or fails to come through for us, we tend to react by showing disappointment or hostility in return. Responding with gentleness is usually much more productive.

8. **Be encouraging!** Youngsters get enough criticism from their peers, from some parents and from some teachers and school officials. Usually what they need most is encouragement. In the long run, positive recognition for an achievement has a lot more reinforcement value than does a put-down for a failure or undesirable action.

9. **Be fun!** Those youth leaders who are most effective are usually fun to be around. They're pleasant, courteous, positive and know how to have a good time. Nothing turns a kid off more quickly than an adult who talks of faith, joy and peace but acts worried, morose and frantic. Relax and enjoy the trip. You'll get more out of it — and so will the young people who travel the road of life with you.

10. **Be enthusiastic!** Your young people will never be more excited about a youth activity than you are. "Nothing great was ever achieved without enthusiasm," said the wise Emerson. *Enthusiasm,* which is defined as *keen interest,* is contagious. A little exposure to it can infect a whole group.

There are many more characteristics of a good youth worker than the 10 I have listed, but these are absolutely essential. I seriously question that a person can become an effective youth worker without making all 10 of them top priorities.

Did you notice that every one of those keys to exerting a positive influence is something that can be cultivated? It's true that some people are born with a temperament that naturally expresses some of those traits, but all of us, with effort, can develop our abilities to demonstrate each of the keys.

I suggest that you go back and read over the list again. As you review them, rate yourself on a scale of one to 10 on each of them, and set a goal for improving each of them that does not rate at least a 10 in your current experience.

Needed: Good Role Models

A high-school football coach recently told a reporter that every boy who steps onto the football field sees himself as another Walter Payton, Ed "Too Tall" Jones or Joe Montana.

In our media-saturated world, more and more young people are seeking to pattern their lives after celebrities. The television camera has become an omnipotent eye that can zero in on a nobody and suddenly transform that insignificant person to national prominence. You need look no further than some model/actresses to see how it works.

Unfortunately, many of the "heroes" which are paraded before the nation's youth have lifestyles that are far from Christian standards. Many rock musicians, actors and athletes flaunt their immorality, and some of them make a lot of money by trying to influence young people to follow the patterns they set.

If you have any doubts as to whether teenagers follow examples set by television personalities, notice how many of these personalities show up on T-shirts youngsters are wearing; notice how many teenagers are wearing designer jeans; and check out the latest statistics on teenage alcoholism. Extensive studies show that television personalities have a significant impact on the attitudes and actions of the typical teenager.

A strong youth leader holds a unique opportunity to help in the shaping of young lives by providing a good example for young people to follow. A real live "hero of the faith" can do much to influence positively the image the typical young person holds of a "true Christian."

Tips for Good Role-Modeling

"Be what you is, 'cause when you is what you ain't, you ain't what you is!" Those words on a sign triggered some thoughts within me on what it means to walk openly and set a good example for the young people with whom I have the privilege of working.

The following tips can help to show you how to set a good example:

1. **Know who you are and what you believe.** I love J.B. Phillips' translation of Romans 12:2. He says, "Don't let the world around you squeeze you into its mold, but let God remold your minds from within."

   Young people usually follow strong individuals — people who know who they are and where they are going in life. They are not impressed by leaders who try to conform to all the ideas others hold about what they should be.

If you are to keep from being "squeezed into the mold" of the world around you, it is necessary that you be able to put into words (if possible, in one short sentence) what you believe and are acting upon. This not only will help you to set a good example, it will provide you with an anchor to hold your life steady during the greatest of storms.

2. Be consistent. In a world where everything is constantly changing, most young people are trying desperately to find something that remains stable. At the same time, there is so much emphasis placed on "relevance" that many youth leaders feel they must be constantly changing to keep up with the latest trends.

Certainly, it is helpful to be alert to changes that are occurring in the youth culture. Nobody wants to be hopelessly outdated. Methods, programming ideas and activities must always reflect new conditions and take advantage of new opportunities.

The consistency of which I speak has more to do with the kind of person you are and the way you treat the youth in your group. More than they need a youth leader who can use correctly all the slang words of their culture, or dress to reflect the latest styles, young people need the steadying hand of a role model who is the same every time they see him or her.

Much has been said in recent years about being honest in expressing your feelings. In other words, always act out the way you feel. That approach might be good for your own mental health, but it can carry with it a price tag in confusion and mistrust among the youth you would lead.

For example, let's say you have scheduled a car wash for a Saturday, and have promoted it like crazy for weeks. Your hope is to make it much more than a fund-raising effort. You want it to be an exercise that will pull together a youth group that has been going in different directions for weeks.

Now, on the day before the car wash, someone offers you an opportunity for the "trip of a lifetime," and you really want to go. You graciously decline because you realize that duty calls.

You go to the car wash with mixed emotions, and, first thing, the troublemakers start trying to pull the group apart. Frustration is the natural human response. "While I'm sitting here baby-sitting this group of spoiled brats, I could be enjoying myself immensely."

It might be honest to express that feeling of frustration, but what's it going to do to your chances of making the day productive as a group exercise? It is a mark of maturity to be able to deal with your own feelings so that what you reflect to the young people in your group is a consistency in the way you treat them.

There's another side to this effort at being consistent — *always be consistent in the way you treat each person in your group.* If you laugh at a behavior in one person, and criticize that same behavior in another, or respond to the antics of a group with laughter one Sunday, only to become angry at the group for the same antics the following week, you can only confuse the youth.

Effective youth leaders learn early that the more consistent they are in the examples they set and in the way they treat the people in their groups, the easier it is to get young people to follow them. They learn to become consistent role models.

3. *Think before you act.* As a free person in a free society, you have a right to act as you choose; but love for those for whom you are role-modeling suggests that you voluntarily put limits on that freedom.

As a leader, personal freedom has to give place to concern for the way the group will interpret your actions.

Let me illustrate with an extreme example. A youth director shared recently that he had had a weekend retreat devastated by one teenaged boy — and his reactions to that boy's behavior. All weekend, the boy had been disruptive and uncooperative. In the closing session, the leader's frustration overcame him, and he slapped the boy across the face.

"It was as if I had slapped the whole group," he later observed. "That entire group had supported me in my efforts to control the boy throughout the weekend, but when I hit him, it was as if they suddenly were in his corner."

It was an immature reaction to the immaturity of a member of the group, and it cost him dearly in the view the others held of him. To a much lesser degree, everything we do as youth leaders is watched carefully by those we would lead. Thus, everything we do becomes important in our efforts to be good role models.

A guiding principle I have found very helpful is expressed in the following question: *Will the proposed action produce the desired result?*

4. ***Show them more than you tell them.*** Preachiness probably closes the door to effective communication with young people more quickly than almost any effort by adult youth leaders.

"A good example is the best sermon," said Ben Franklin in *Poor Richard's Almanac.* To that, Emerson added, "I'd rather see a sermon than hear one any day."

The typical young person is a lot more likely to pay attention to actions that reflect the Sermon on the Mount than to listen to even the most creative efforts to teach the principles it sets forth.

A friend of mine once told me of an incident that occurred when his children were small. The family was sitting together one night, each quietly pursuing his separate interest. Suddenly, there was a loud clap of lightning nearby, and the lights flickered.

"As I lowered the book I was reading," he said, "I noticed that every eye in the room was fixed squarely on me. They were watching to see how I reacted."

That father quietly said, "Let's bring out the candles; the lights might go out." Soon everyone was busily resuming his or her activities and calmly riding out the storm that followed. What the children needed was a demonstration of calm assurance that they could cope with the storm, not a sermon about how God would take care of them.

Youth leaders are more like gardeners than sculptors. The sculptor takes a hammer and chisel and seeks to knock away the rough edges of the stone before them. Their goal is to make that stone look like they want it to look. But young people are not made of stone. They are more like tender plants that need to be nurtured and encouraged to grow.

If we would like to see the youth in our groups grow to maturity in their Christian faith, the greatest thing we can do is demonstrate to them how it is done by the way we live out our lives before them. That has more impact than the strongest sermons we could give.

5. **Lead, don't follow.** Often there is a great difference in being liked and being respected as a leader.

Young people look to their peers to wander around with them in their adolescent lifestyles. They like to get together and talk their jargon; they like to dress alike; and they want to share their discoveries of the mysteries of life with people who are making similar discoveries. But they are like the blind leading the blind around in circles.

What they need from adults, and what many of them secretly want, is leadership. They need to be led toward adulthood by a role model who can understand where they are, but can stimulate them to become something they have not yet been.

The story is told of a man who worked in a large office tower in a major city. This man often dreamed of owning a bearskin coat, and he knew that the only way he'd ever get it was to kill a bear and have his own coat made. On his vacation, he went to the mountains, armed and ready, to kill a bear.

Presently he came upon a bear who was sitting outside his cave, trying to get his senses collected after his long winter's sleep. The office worker raised his gun, aimed, and was about to pull the trigger when the old bear threw up his paw and said, "Wait a minute! Let's negotiate about this thing!"

"What do you mean, 'negotiate'?" the man replied.

"Welll," drawled the old bear, "you want a fur coat, and I'm hungry! We might be able to help each other."

"Keep talking," said the man.

"Let's go inside my cave so we can talk more privately," invited the bear.

Two hours later, the old bear emerged licking his lips. You see, he had gotten his meal, and the man was surrounded by a nice bearskin coat. But in the process, the man had lost his identity!

That's a silly fable, yet it illustrates what happens to many youth leaders who try in every way possible to become like the young people they would lead. They are completely accepted by the youngsters, but they lose their own identity; at least they lose that which sets them apart as adults — that which makes them good role models.

Finding that balance between being like the youth you would lead and providing a role model they can follow is often a confusing task. I have always found the following principle helpful in fulfilling that task: *Accept the young people you would lead — exactly as they are — and give them an example of what they can become.*

Cashing in on that Unique Opportunity

As youth leaders, we all have a golden opportunity — an opportunity that almost no one else has — to play a vital role in the shaping of young lives.

To take advantage of that opportunity, we need the spirit reflected by the elderly teacher who always bowed before his students on the first day of each semester to recognize what those students might someday become.

I like Dr. Robert Schuller's saying: "Anyone can count the seeds in an apple, but only God can count the apples in a seed." If we might fit that saying to our situation, we could say, "Any person can see the problems young people can create, but only a loving and creative youth leader can see the potential they contain."

An effective youth leader is one who guides, stimulates and encourages young people to become all that they were created to be. To do that, a leader must play many roles: teacher, facilitator, friend, spiritual confidant and stimulator.

Everything about us communicates something to the youth in our groups. If we would take advantage of the unique opportunities we have to help shape lives, we must constantly be aware that our attitudes show through our actions, that we have the power to influence, and that we are role models for the young people who present themselves to us week after week.

GROWTH EXERCISE

Take a few moments and write a brief answer for each of the following questions:

1. **What is my** *primary* **motivation for entering or being in youth work?**

2. **What do I do regularly to assure that the influence I hold over the young people in my group is a positive influence?**

3. **What are my goals for becoming a better role model for the youth in my group?**

4. **Which dominates my thinking and preparation for programs and activities:**

   a. My own self-image and desires?

   b. The needs and concerns of the young people I seek to lead?

5. **Would I like the young people in my group to become like me? Why?**

CHAPTER 2

Youth Ministry in Perspective

Three blind men were once asked to "view" an elephant, and to describe the huge animal.

"The elephant is flat, rather like a wall," said the first. He had been led to the side of the elephant and felt its large stomach.

"No," said the second. "It is rather like a tree." He had "viewed" the elephant by feeling its large leg.

"Both are wrong," insisted the third blind man. "The elephant is long and slender — rather like a snake." He had felt the elephant's tail.

They had all described the same animal from the particular perspective they had. Each was correct, yet each was incorrect, for he had only viewed the elephant from a very limited perspective.

Poll the members of a typical church to find out how they view the role of youth ministry in the broader scope of the church's life, and you will get as many different perspectives as there are members.

Balancing Differing Expectations

Whether you will be effective as a youth director might very well hinge on how effectively you balance the wide range of expectations and definitions of the role of youth ministry within your church or group.

Many youth directors are frustrated, unhappy and ineffective because they operate under completely unrealistic expectations from the youth, parents, church leaders and the congregation. Their misery is often compounded by the fact that they, themselves, have unrealistic expectations.

Unrealistic Expectations from Church

It might be helpful to take a look at some of the more common faulty expectations:

Police Officer: In many churches the youth director is seen as the police officer in charge of the children.

Some youth directors are given instructions by the leaders of the church to "keep the children entertained" while the grownups get on with the worship, learning and the running of church business.

What youth director has not encountered a situation like this? Johnny is a terror at his junior-high school, a disaster at home, and a constant enemy at play. He is brought to youth programs with the admonition of his parents to "make him behave." Of course, they never say how.

Now Johnny may want to roam the halls, damage the building, disrupt everything going on and generally make a nuisance of himself. He must be controlled so that he does not disturb the adults, injure the other children, or vandalize the building and grounds.

Who is expected to do all this controlling? You guessed it — the youth director. And he or she is expected to do it without strait jackets, inflicting bodily harm (however tempting that may be), or offending the parents of the little "overly energetic fellow."

Furthermore, the youth director should not only keep the children under control while they are involved in youth activities, but should teach them to respect the worship service. They must be taught to sit up straight, listen, be quiet and pay tithes.

And if the youth director really does a good job, none of the children will get into trouble in the community. After all, as everyone knows, "Children brought up in church are seldom brought up in court."

Finally, as police officer, the youth leader is expected to arbitrate disputes among the children with the wisdom of Solomon, the patience of Job and the gentleness of Miriam — even though he or she may feel like using the tactics of Elisha, who called out the she-bears on an unruly crowd of children.

Of course, the youth director can be expected to maintain order and teach respect for the church and the community. However, if that becomes the primary focus of the job, that youth director is whipped before he or she starts.

It is absolutely crucial that church leaders and parents not abdicate their responsibilities in the area of discipline; that the youth director have the backing of the church in matters of discipline; and that the children see him or her as friendly as well as authoritarian.

Teacher: In some churches the youth program is seen as consisting of the funnel approach to filling the heads of the young people with Bible knowledge. It works like this:

Picture the Bible as a five-gallon can with a spout for pouring, the contents of the can as facts and Scripture references, and the youth director as the "fueler."

In this scenario, the youth director bores a hole in the heads of the youngsters while making them think it is fun. Then he or she inserts a funnel which we may call "teaching techniques." Now, each youngster's head is filled with Bible knowledge so that he or she can spout out Scriptures and facts in rapid-fire succession.

Of course, there are some problems. First of all, the Bible can be studied for a lifetime and still leave many questions unanswered. Secondly, the youngster seldom views the process as fun and more often would rather be throwing spitballs. Thirdly, the whole method was abandoned long ago by the schools because it was ineffective. Fourthly, the study of the Bible necessarily involves a commitment on the part of students and must be made alive in the arena where they spend their daily life.

It is realistic for the church to expect the youth director to create frameworks within which the youth can study the Bible. However, it is also the youth leader's responsibility to clarify for the church the role of parents and church leaders, the opportunities they have in this area, the relationship of the Bible to the total life situation of the youth, and the development of the youth as full participating members of the church.

Social Director: In many churches the youth director is stereotyped as the social director. The primary task is defined as helping the young people work off all that energy with constructive activities.

On a budget that is almost nonexistent, the leader must come up with "fun things" for the kids to do which will compete with television shows that are produced at a cost of millions, compete with amusement parks that draw people from all over the world, and challenge movies that pay millions to get professional actors to perform.

We live in an entertainment-oriented society which will pay a publicly immoral quarterback a cool million to throw passes and call plays, surround him with the best personnel, and give him topnotch coaching and the best equipment, while grumbling about spending peanuts on developing the spiritual lives of its children.

Not only must youth directors in some churches keep the children entertained, they must do it without interfering with homework, school and family functions, and with a constantly changing crowd.

Furthermore, if they do a good job, the youngsters entrusted to their care will emerge with all the social graces. They will not pick their noses in public, whisper in church or poke fun at other people.

Any church that looks to its youth director as entertainer or social director is sure to be disappointed, and any youth director who takes on this challenge might do well to consider the profession of acting instead of youth ministry.

Entertainment and social activities are an important part of an effective youth ministry, but they are not all that is involved. Again, it is the responsibility of the youth director to constantly bring this into focus for the church.

One further note — in some churches, the opposite is true. Some people seem to feel that entertainment has no valid place in the church's ministry to its youth. Maintaining a healthy balance between too much and too little fun is a real challenge for the person who most often stands in the middle ground between a church and its youth.

Salesperson: Quite often the church looks to its youth director as the person responsible for convincing the young people that they ought to support the church financially and in attendance, that they should become missionaries or other professional church workers, and that they ought to be good at home. This, according to some, should be done without being preachy.

The young people tend to relate to the youth director as their salesperson to convince the church that they need money for their activities, that they ought to be given permission to do things they desire, and that the church should provide more and require less.

This orientation robs the church of one of its most exciting possibilities, casts the youth director in an impossible role, and usually results in a failure to adequately sell anything to anybody. While it is true that selling is an important part of the youth director's job, careful attention must be given to what is to be sold and to whom.

A more realistic view of the youth director is that of a facilitator who enables the church and its youth to communicate values and needs to each other.

Evangelist: Some churches view the youth director as an evangelist whose primary responsibility is to get the young people converted. This, of course, must be done without an overemphasis on emotionalism and without making fanatics of them.

If a youth director is on the ball, they say, he or she will bring in lots of "nice" young people to the church and scare the teenagers enough to keep them from having premarital sex, smoking cigarettes, drinking beer and using drugs.

The problem with this view is that it tends to simultaneously make too much and too little of the youth director.

While the conversion experience and nurture of spiritual growth ought to be uppermost in the mind of the youth director, it is too big a task for one person. Again, the youth director must focus for the entire church and the parents of its youth the challenges and opportunities of providing for spiritual well-being of its youth.

Substitute Pastor: In some churches the youth director is seen as a substitute pastor, who is expected to visit and counsel with those people whom the pastor does not have the time to see.

Many problems that ought to be handled by the pastor are referred to the youth director because they involve young people.

Any youth director who assumes undue responsibilities in this area is likely to be frustrated and to participate in a failure of the church to adequately meet the needs of its members.

Most youth problems are little more than a symptom of family problems. The youth director is not likely to have the training, experience or skills to deal effectively with such situations.

"After all," some parents argue, "it is the youth director who has the best contact with our son."

The problem that this idea holds is apparent on the surface. The parents are viewing the problem as someone else's and not their own.

Some guidelines for not getting typed as a substitute pastor are:

- Always consult with the church's pastor before and after any counseling situation.

- When counseling is indicated, view yourself as part of a team of counselors and suggest that parents talk with the pastor. If possible, get the family as a whole to talk with you and the pastor together so that roles may be clarified.

● Learn to recognize when you are in over your head and scream for help. After consulting with your pastor, refer deeply troubled teenagers and their parents to competent Christian professional counselors.

Developing a positive attitude toward your role and cultivating a healthy set of expectations within the leadership and membership of your church is vital if you are to be effective as a minister to youth. A big part of this task is to overcome the false expectations of your role. These false notions are seldom stated and usually are not overt attempts by anyone to hamper your effectiveness.

I suggest that you approach the whole process creatively and positively early in your ministry so that it will not have to be dealt with in frustration and anger later.

Your Own Unrealistic Expectations

Add to the unrealistic expectations most churches hold for the youth leaders the idealistic notions many people bring to the task, and you have a real formula for ulcers.

As a frequent airline passenger, I've learned that there are only so many things I can take onboard with me — without being billed for "excess baggage." It might be helpful to take a look at some of the "excess baggage" many youth leaders bring to the task with them, and some of the "extra charges" it costs them. Many youth directors see themselves as:

All Things to All People: Many youth leaders take seriously the varied demands placed on them by all the people who have an impact on their lives. *After all,* they reason, *the church is paying my salary (or is expecting me to do a good job as a volunteer), and I must convince them I am worthy of their confidence.*

It works just fine until the expectations of various people or groups begin to conflict with each other — which is usually about the end of the first week.

A real-life example can serve to illustrate how a youth director can get caught in hopeless situations. Believe me, this really happened to a full-time youth director in Georgia.

He had set aside a day for planning an upcoming retreat. The night before his planning date, the "head deacon" from the church called him and asked if he could fill in as a speaker at a civic club meeting the next day. The scheduled speaker had cancelled out at the last minute. He agreed. Early on the day of planning, he went to the church office and started to work. Soon the church secretary buzzed him and told him there had been an accident, one of the members had been rushed to the hospital, and the pastor was out of town. He agreed to rush down to the hospital. He had just returned and started to prepare some remarks for his noon luncheon when the intercom buzzed again. This time, it was a parent who was "in an emergency situation" with her child and needed help right away. He agreed to stop by on the way to the luncheon. When he got there, the "emergency" was all taken care of. It had been a fight, and the conflict had been settled by the mother sending the girl to her room.

On his way to his car, the youth director was thinking about his goals that had been pushed aside for what had turned out to be a day of putting out brush fires. Just as he reached the car, he was faced with the straw that broke the camel's back.

"Hey, Jim," called the mother with the so-called emergency, "Charles has the car today, and I'm trying to bake a cake. Will you stop by the store on your way back and bring me a bottle of vanilla extract?"

You will find, if you have not already found, that trying to be all things to all people can devastate your efforts at youth ministry and give you an ulcer. Most people think their requests are very realistic. There's always the parent who wants you to "sneak up on" a son or daughter and talk them into or out of something, or the youngster who wants you to take part in a cover-up, or the church leader who thinks the youth should raise funds to pave the parking lot.

A youth leader must, of course, work with all people as effectively as possible. However, the leader who tries to become all things to all people is likely to end up being nothing to anybody.

The only hope of coping effectively with the tremendous demands others seek to place on you is to maintain a clearly defined set of goals — both personally and in your youth program — and stick to the pursuit of those goals as rigidly as possible. I will have much more to say about how to do this in a later chapter.

Rescuer/Redeemer/Hero: Your image of yourself as a youth director is usually shaped by role models you have observed as you have grown up. You tend to try to be like those people who have influenced your life.

But there's a tricky thing about the way we tend to view role models. We usually don't pick just one, and try to follow that person's example; we put together a composite image of several people we have known, and try to emulate the best characteristics of all of them.

One of the traits youth directors most frequently try to copy is that of rescuer, or redeemer or hero. We hate to see someone hurt, so we try to rush in to solve all of that person's problems.

When it comes to young people, most of us adults tend to be "fixers." You've seen the type — maybe you are the type! A girl in the group gets pregnant, comes to the youth director for help, and the youth director takes over to solve the problem. Or a guy gets arrested, and the youth leader tries to get the police to drop the charges.

The biggest problem with trying to play the hero is that it doesn't work.

These principles have always been helpful to me in drawing the line on how far I should go in trying to be helpful to young people and their parents:

- Understand that people have both the resources and the responsibility to solve their own problems.

- Understand that facing consequences is a necessary ingredient for growth.

- Understand that solutions imposed from the outside not only are seldom effective, but rob the involved people of the benefits of their own struggles.

- Understand that there is only one Redeemer — Jesus Christ.

One veteran youth minister said, "The great freedom to minister to hurting people came when I realized the difference between being redeemer, and being redemptive. I cannot redeem anyone . . . only Christ can do that. But I can be redemptive in that I can assist people in finding their own solutions through him."

Surrogate Parent: Many pastors have told me that one of the greatest problems they have had with youth directors is that they sometimes try to become substitute parents for the young people in their groups. They offer a great deal of advice, constantly chide youngsters about everything from the people they date to doing their homework, and generally try to take over the role of parenting.

The temptation is often the greatest when the youngster's parents are not Christians or when the youth director feels the teenager is not getting enough attention at home.

When youth leaders are too directive in interfering with the personal lives of young people, they often find themselves in conflict with parents, seeking to influence youngsters to choose for themselves and driving members of their group away by being too nosy.

Youth leaders who know who they are and understand the role they fulfill, can make a valuable contribution to the lives of the children and young people who are entrusted to them.

One of the Crowd: Everybody likes to be accepted, and most youth directors are not exceptions to that rule. However, sometimes that urge can become overpowering and we find ourselves trying to be one of the kids.

Teenagers are cute with their fads, their jargon and their flighty mannerisms. But an adult trying to act like a teenager looks silly — especially to the teenagers.

Young people have plenty of peers. In fact, they may often have too many peers — or at least may be influenced too much by their peers. What they really need from a youth leader is the steadying influence of an adult who understands the confusing cross-signals they get from all the many types of peers they encounter.

An old political slogan expressed this idea of leadership very well. A candidate was described as "a voice, not just an echo!"

The shepherds in Middle Eastern countries have learned that sheep will follow pretty much where they are led. If they are not led, they will just wander around aimlessly, and eventually fall victim to the wolves. Often the shepherds use a goat as an "assistant shepherd." The sheep think the goat is one of them, and will follow him anywhere — even to the slaughterhouse.

Do you know what they call that goat? They call it a Judas goat, because it leads the sheep to their own deaths. What young people need are not Judas goats, but real shepherds who will care for them and lead them to become something they have not yet been.

Wise Sage: Some of us who set out to become youth directors approach the task as if we are wise sages who have amassed a tremendous amount of savvy about what life is like in the real world. We like to dump our great wisdom on any who will dare listen, and wonder why young people are not asking the questions we are trying to answer.

The wise sage uses phrases like, "You're wrong," or "That's foolish," or "Let me tell you how it was when I was your age!" When the youth in our groups are more fascinated by Pac-Man or by listening to their stereos than they are by hearing our words of wisdom, we get frustrated and feel rejected.

Do you remember that famous line from the movie *Murder by Death*? The Chinese detective said of the proposed solution to the crime, "Only one thing wrong with theory — is stupid . . . is most stupid theory I ever heard!"

I wouldn't go quite that far. However, truly wise men have been lamenting for centuries the fact that young people are not willing to readily accept the wisdom of a previous generation. As much as we'd like to change things, most growing people still have to learn for themselves. And they tend to learn more by experience than by absorbing imparted wisdom.

It can save you a lot of headaches to realize that you will probably always be more serious about imparting what you have learned than the youth in your group will be about receiving it.

Super-Grouper: Most of us start out with the idea that we are going to have the biggest, best and most exciting youth group the world has ever known. When it doesn't happen almost overnight, we begin experiencing feelings of failure. Sometimes we try to ease our disappointment by blaming other people or circumstances.

Some of the most effective and the happiest youth leaders I have known have told me they realized early that building a good youth group is a slow and tedious process. It is one that requires a great deal of patience and persistence.

Super-groupers tend to burn out early, to become discouraged and to settle for something less than they could be.

Those who make their mark in youth work generally are the ones who set their goals somewhat, but not too far, above the achievements of the previous year, then work steadily to achieve those goals. They're more like the tortoise than the rabbit in the famous fable. They steadily plod along, take setbacks in stride, receive victories as bonuses, and work toward worthwhile goals.

What Is an Effective Youth Director?

Before we seek to define the role of the youth director, it might be helpful to clarify the role of youth ministry within the church:

An effective youth ministry in the local church is one that brings out the full resources of all its members, leaders and staff to assist its youth in reaching their full potential as a group and as individuals in their relationships with God, their families, the church and the world around them, and reaches out to the young people in its area with the good news of our Lord Jesus Christ.

Scripturally, the task of the church as it relates to its youth is to seek to bring every person to " . . . mature manhood, measured by nothing less than the full stature of Christ." (Ephesians 4:13, New English Bible) With this assisting in mind, let us proceed to attempt a definition of what the youth director ought to be doing and how he or she should be doing it.

A Realistic View of the Role of Youth Director

As Person: Someone has observed that it has been several decades since the youth of this nation have recognized an undisputed national hero. This is probably true.

In fact, the emphasis has shifted from hero worship to a concern for relationships. This is probably one of the healthiest changes that has occurred in our society in many years.

What it means to you as a youth director is that your effectiveness will depend in large measure on the depth, nature and quality of the relationships you will be able to establish and maintain with your church and its youth. More specifically, it means that most the valuable asset you bring to your ministry among youth is you, as a person. Unfortunately, this is the area that is most often neglected. Too many youth directors see themselves — and are seen by their churches — as more important because of what they do than what they are.

This is evidenced by the fact that so many youth ministers are overworked and spend so little time on personal development and spiritual growth. A day off to rest and have fun, time spent in prayer and reading, attending retreats and maintaining family relationships are not luxuries; they are essentials.

The way you see yourself and the way others see you, as a person, is so vital that nothing — absolutely nothing — is as important as being all that you can through Christ.

You will have an impact on the young people whose lives you touch that will be far more influential by the kind of person you are and the way the Gospel manifests itself in your life than by anything you will ever say. Young people tend to pattern their lives after what sociologists call role models. The way you set your priorities, shape your relationships and cope with crises will do more to influence the spiritual development of your church's youth than anything you do in programming.

Perhaps most important of all are the friendships that grow up through your contact with young people. In this age of alienation and depersonalization, one of the most valuable assets that church can offer is the friendship of a person like you.

The Youth Director as Guide: The adolescent years have been described as turbulent, frightening and lonely. It is that period of life when the transition is made from childhood to maturity. It is necessarily a time of probing, questioning, searching, experimenting, challenging, learning and testing.

Adolescence is also a very exciting time for the teenager and the adult worker who is invited along for the trip. Most teenagers welcome along on their journey someone who is willing to serve as guide. However, most of them reject anyone who seeks merely to cram them into a preconceived mold.

As guide, you can share in and lead the search; you can assist in the development of values; you can lead to new discoveries and experiences.

The Youth Director as Coordinator, Motivator and Facilitator: The term *director* implies that the person does not do everything, but rather enables other people to do all the things necessary to bring to bear the full resources of the church in its efforts to assist its youth's growth in Christ. There are several ways in which the youth director can do this:

● He can act as a coordinator for the church in its efforts to define, plan and implement its youth ministry.

I cannot overemphasize the importance of the church's role in assessing the needs of its youth and developing strategies to meet those needs. In our efforts to become specialized, we often overlook some very basic principles of group dynamics.

The concept of hiring a professional to "take over our youth program" is often an effort by the church to deny its responsibilities in this area.

"You're the professional! What do you think we should do?" is another trap. It may be flattering to be asked, but if you and the church do not understand the way they view the needs of their youth and the strategies for meeting those needs, sooner or later there will be serious conflict.

At worst, the church will misunderstand what you are trying to do or your methods for doing it. At the least, you will not utilize the resources available to you.

Coordinate in whatever ways you can. Bring out the best potential of your church for meeting the needs of its youth.

● The youth director can work to train, motivate, equip and guide adults and youth workers. Those youth ministries that are most effective are the ones in which the workers are sure what is expected of them and are confidently excited about fulfilling their tasks. Such preparation is the responsibility of the youth director.

● The youth director can facilitate the flow of ideas and information from all levels of the church to their proper place. It is not nearly so important that the youth director translate the thinking of the youth to the pastor or official board and vice versa as it is that he or she create a framework through which they can talk openly to each other. Once the young people and the church get together on what they would like to have by way of youth ministry and commit themselves to achieving it, your job is exciting.

● The youth director can also serve to integrate young people into the mainstream of the church. Young people have so much to give to the life and vitality of the church and the church has so much to offer its youth that one of the youth director's main tasks is to constantly seek ways to bring them together in a creative search and at the point of ministry.

The Youth Director as Resource Person: If the youth director has a bag of tricks, it is in the realm of ideas and information. The person who is learning and growing constantly and is forever making exciting new discoveries can prove a valuable resource for the local church.

Reading, attending seminars and talking to successful people is as important to the youth director in staying abreast of the lastest techniques of ministry as staying up on the latest surgical practices is to the brain surgeon.

It is not enough, however, to simply know what's happening. The youth director must find ways of keeping the decision-makers in the church informed.

One youth director recently complained that while almost all his ideas had been rejected by his former church, as soon as he left, they were all put into practice. He had developed a great set of ideas but had fallen down in translating them to the proper people.

A youth director who doesn't care who gets the credit for ideas will not only have a going youth ministry, but will always be in demand.

The Youth Director as Enabler: In the Bible, the terms *minister* and *servant* are often used interchangeably. In fact, Jesus said that he who would be greatest must become servant of all.

One reason youth work tends to drain directors is that they are always giving out and never receiving. This one-way flow of ministry not only conditions the young people to always expect to receive instead of give, it robs them of the opportunity to grow up in the Lord and deprives the youth minister of a valuable source of life. Those who would minister must be willing to be ministered unto.

Helping people minister to each other is a vital function of the alert youth director.

Providing for the nurture of the "new babes in Christ" is another one of those areas in which the youth director is an enabler. Making it easier for new Christians to work into the group and for the group to accept them is a real challenge for the youth director.

Perhaps the greatest asset in this business of enabling is the ability to accept people as they are — with all their capabilities and hang-ups. Recognizing the capabilities of young people and adult workers and bringing those abilities up to maximum fruition is the stock in trade of the youth director. Likewise, the leader must be able to accept the limitations and failures of people without becoming judgmental.

The Youth Director as Inspirer and Encourager: It is always interesting to me to see high-school and college students call the director of a play to the stage between acts to give him an award and express their appreciation to him. Actually, all the director has done is give the actors the courage to try and the coaching to make them succeed. Maybe the message is that anybody likes someone who sees his capabilities and helps in his development.

Helping people unlock their talents is a never-ending and sometimes frustrating task, but is always worth the effort. "Go ahead, you can do it" ranks second only to "I love you" in key phrases for the effective youth director.

GROWTH EXERCISE

We've talked about some unrealistic expectations that various groups within the church hold for the youth leader, some excess baggage that some of us bring to the task of leading youth, and about some realistic views of what a youth director should expect to be able to give and to receive in return. The following exercise can help you to focus for yourself just what you expect to bring to, and receive from, your role as a youth leader.

Spend a few minutes writing out an answer to each of the following questions:

1. **List at least one person who had a significant impact on you while you were growing up. What traits did you see in that person that made you want to be like him or her? What shortcomings would you like to avoid?**

2. **List at least five things you would like to be able to offer to the group in your church.**

3. **List at least five expectations you have for things you would like to receive from your youth work.**

4. **Write a one-sentence description of yourself as a youth leader.**

CHAPTER 3

What Does It Take to Be an Effective Youth Leader?

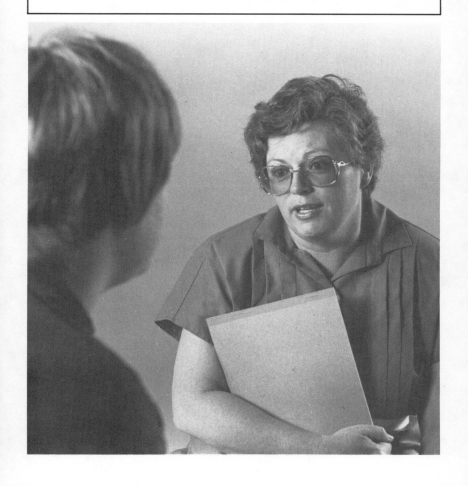

Why do some churches have dynamic and exciting youth ministries, while the youth ministries of other churches just seem to drag along?

The answer to that question, I believe, lies within the following statement: *The key ingredient of an effective youth ministry is an effective youth leader.*

Let's face it — some youth directors are winners, others are losers. How can you tell the difference? During many years of working with church youth programs and youth-serving agencies all over the world, I have seen some of both — winners and losers. Here are some of the differences I have noticed:

- Winners make their goals; losers make excuses.

- Winners take advantage of opportunities; losers complain about problems.

- Winners get life sorted out and know where they're going; losers ramble all over the place.

- Winners concentrate on planning; losers concentrate on activity.

- Winners motivate and guide other people; losers criticize.

- Winners fix problems; losers fix the blame.

- Winners understand others; losers seek understanding.

"Some people have it and some people don't" is the view of many. I totally disagree. Most of the successful youth leaders I have known will tell you that they have had to work hard at developing the traits that make them successful.

In this chapter, I'd like to give you 10 marks of an effective youth leader. As you look at each, realize that it is a trait you can develop, or if you already have it, you can improve on it.

An Effective Youth Leader
Is Enthusiastic

Young people are full of life, excitement and action. They like to follow enthusiastic people.

Enthusiasm is defined as *great fervor, a strong commitment,* and *an air of excitement.* By those definitions, how enthusiastic are you?

"But I don't feel enthusiastic, and I can't fake it," a young woman said to me after a seminar for youth workers. I reminded her of Dale Carnegie's famous analogy: "It is easier to act your way into feeling than to feel your way into action." In other words, if you don't believe in what you are doing and can't bring yourself to believe in what you are doing, you need to get out of youth work. If you believe in what you are doing, act like you believe in it.

When you act enthusiastic, two very big things happen:

First: You begin to feel enthusiastic! Try it! The next time you are presenting an idea or giving a talk, concentrate on selling that idea as if it were the most important thing in the world to you at that moment. You will feel enthusiasm beginning to take hold of you, and soon you will enjoy what you are doing.

Second: You will see others begin to feel enthusiastic! "Enthusiasm is contagious." It's an old saying, but it is more true now than ever. Notice sometime how those TV announcers present their automobile commercials. They'd have you believe that the cars they're selling are the greatest thing since sliced bread. Do you know why they do that? It works! People get excited about what they're being told because the announcers are excited.

Remember this: the youth in your group will never be one bit more enthusiastic than you are.

An Effective Youth Leader Has
a Positive Mental Attitude

Someone once defined *play* as *doing what you enjoy.* If you enjoy young people, if you have planned your time carefully enough to avoid the pressure of too much to do, and know how to get the backing of your church, you can have a great deal of fun as a youth director.

Take it from me, you will never have enough resources, an ideal working situation, or all the cooperation you desire. Success in youth work does not depend on the absence of problems; it depends on what you do with the problems you encounter.

Earl Nightingale is right: "Every problem presents an equal or greater opportunity." The loser focuses attention on the problem and complains about it. The winner takes seriously the old saying, "If life gives you a lemon, make lemonade."

The director of a junior-high camp once shared with me how the lemonade theory averted a near-disaster in her most recent camp. About noon on the third day of camp, a girl became ill and was taken to the camp doctor. He checked her over, diagnosed the problem as a viral infection, and suggested the girl be sent home to check the virus's spread. By 3 that afternoon, about a dozen girls were reporting feeling bad. The doctor rushed out to the camp, checked each of the girls and determined that none of the girls had symptoms of the virus. By 8 that evening, two-thirds of the girls in the camp were "sick." Mass hysteria had broken out, and rumors about all kinds of fatal diseases were flying everywhere.

The camp director called a hasty staff meeting, and several staff members were suggesting they close the camp.

"I've got an idea," said a cagey old counselor who'd been through many such episodes. She presented her plan, the nurse called the doctor and cleared it with him, and they set about to cure the "epidemic."

The girls were all lined up outside the dispensary. One at a time, they came in and the nurse gave them a large yellow pill, each girl getting the same instructions: "Open wide, drink this water, swallow the pill, and go directly to bed. The pill will make you sleepy, but it will cure it if you've got it or make you immune if you haven't caught it yet." The counselors herded the girls off to bed, enforced absolute silence, and soon the girls were all fast asleep.

Next morning, the girls were all "well," excited, and curious about what was in the "miracle pill." No one ever told them that the nurse had had to go through 10 large packs of M & M's to get enough yellow "pills" for each of the girls to have one.

Not all emergencies can be averted so easily, but the positive approach always results in better solutions than does the negative.

A Good Leader Knows How to Communicate Effectively

There is a lot of competition for the attention of young people today. Radio, television, videogames, movies, other young people and a host of other voices are crying out for their attention. If you expect to compete, you must learn how to communicate *effectively*.

Communication basically involves a two-way flow of information. It is not enough to always be sending messages. Careful attention must be given to the messages the young people are sending back to you. Listening and observing are as much a part of effective communication as is talking. Hearing the questions your young people are asking is the first step in giving them the answers they are seeking.

I will give some definite pointers on how to communicate effectively with young people in a later chapter.

An Effective Youth Leader
Is a Loving Person

Young people become interested in people who are interested in them. They can spot a phony a mile away.

Have you ever told a deeply troubling problem to someone, and had that person respond as if they thought it was silly for you to even worry about such a thing? The teenager who works up the courage to talk with you about where he or she is hurting is looking for understanding — not the brush-off. The youth leader who cares and understands the needs and concerns of young people can expect them to respond positively to his or her concerns.

I am not suggesting that you simply throw around the phrase *I love you*. It might be helpful for you to write out a definition of what you mean when you say *I love you* to a group of young people.

To be understood, love must become very tangible. It is almost as important to look for tangible ways to demonstrate love as it is to love. You do that by taking seriously every member of your group, by going the extra mile in seeing that their needs are met, and by treating all people with dignity and respect.

An Effective Youth Leader Has
Courage and Integrity

Sometimes, as a youth leader, you will be confronted with situations in which you must act with courage. You might have to take an unpopular stand with your youth group, or with the leaders of your church.

Challenging patterns and programs that have been around a long time and are no longer effective can be hazardous to your standing with certain people. Making sure that your young people always get a fair shake from the church leaders, insisting that young people live up to their obligations, and dealing with young people who constantly challenge your authority can all be thorny problems.

Every effort should be made to avoid open conflict, and confrontation must always be done with love and gentleness. However, both young people and adults will respect the person who has enough courage to stand up for what he or she believes is right — even if they disagree with that person's stand.

One caution: The brand of courage I am describing is not the bulldog fearlessness that causes a person to run around with a chip on his shoulder waiting for someone to knock it off. It is rather the ability to overcome fear and either act, or refuse to act, when an important issue is involved.

Likewise, integrity is a necessary trait for the person who would lead youth. Young people learn to respect and trust the leader they can always count upon. They look for those who always keep their promises, who back up their claims with their daily lives, and whose loyalty can be counted upon when others are attacking them.

"If I'm not present, who will speak for me?" represents an old tradition. It holds that integrity means a person will always represent the best interests of a friend — regardless of whether the friend is present or absent.

Gossip has wrecked more youth directors' ministries than you can imagine. It starts out with one member of the group coming to tell the leader a juicy tale about another member. If that leader joins in attacking the absent person, others will join in. Pretty soon the leaders will notice that everyone in the group is talking with them about the actions of others, but that no one is talking with them about their own problems, needs or concerns. Why? The young people figure that if the youth director will criticize others behind their backs, he or she will also criticize them when they are not present.

There is no position that requires more honesty, trustworthiness or sincerity than that of youth leader. Courage and integrity are absolute musts if you would be an effective youth leader.

An Effective Youth Leader Is Courteous and Considerate

A healthy respect for other people is best reflected by courtesy and consideration of the other person's feelings.

Young people have a way of preying on the weaknesses of one or two members of the group. They might ride one person constantly about a handicap, a large nose or a weight problem. The leader who is concerned with winning popularity contests might be tempted to join in the "good-natured" teasing and taunting of the victim. It is a trap from which there is no escape. Not only can it do irreparable emotional harm to the victim, it creates the feeling among other members of the group that the leader cannot be trusted to come to their aid if they ever need him or her.

Adolescents are bundles of feelings. They usually operate at extreme levels: they are either afire with excitement or down in the dumps. Sometimes the slightest word or action by a youth leader can trigger reactions that are far out of proportion to what the leader expected. Consideration can not only save you a lot of hassle, it can protect those tender feelings from unnecessary hurt.

Courtesy involves treating all people with dignity and respect, the way Jesus treated people. It stems from a recognition that all people have value to God.

Do you consider yourself a courteous person? Are you considerate of the needs and feelings of other people? The way you answer those questions may have a big impact on how well you will do as a youth leader.

An Effective Youth Leader Is Grateful

I have enjoyed a great deal of success as a professional speaker. Once, when I was feeling very confident about my success, I awoke one morning with a bad case of laryngitis. No matter how hard I tried, I couldn't speak above a whisper — and I had an important speaking engagement scheduled for later that morning.

As I sat there in that lonely hotel room and thought about what life would be like if I could never speak again, I realized that my greatest asset — my voice — was a gift from God. Right then, I dropped to my knees and thanked him for all he had given me. I've never taken that gift lightly again.

We human beings have a strange twist to our nature — the more we receive, the easier it is for us to take our gifts for granted. In fact, some of the most ungrateful people I have ever met have been people who had had much given to them. How many people have you seen give thanks when they have a flat tire? Instead of being grateful for three tires that are not flat, or being happy that we have not had more flat tires than we have, we tend to become angry and complain about the one flat we do get.

It works that way in youth ministry, too. It's easy to get upset about rain "spoiling" a retreat for us, rather than to be grateful for the roof we have over our heads to protect us from the rain. It's easy to be frustrated by the budget limitations placed upon us, rather than to be grateful for the money we are given for our work.

Gratitude is one of the great graces of life. No task is greater for the youth leader than that of inspiring a sense of gratitude in the hearts of young people. You can only inspire that sense of gratitude when you are truly grateful for the things you receive.

Often, when things are not going my way, I find it helpful to make a list of all the things for which I'm grateful. It's amazing how much better things look to me as I count my blessings.

An Effective Youth Leader Is Dedicated

"We are not placed on this earth to do anything that we cannot do with our whole heart," a wise old sage once said. Nowhere is that more true than in shaping the lives of young people.

If your reasons for being a youth leader fall into the category of "a sense of obligation to my church," or "because there was no one else to do it," or "I have the talent for it, and I've got to have a job," I doubt seriously that you will become a very effective youth leader.

Youth work often involves long hours, difficult circumstances, complaining followers and church leaders, and little or no pay. Those who become involved without making the total commitment find it frustrating and draining.

On the other hand, those people who are dedicated to Christ, to their church, and to the all-important task of building young lives find it to be a rich and rewarding experience. They find that they can inspire young people to commit their lives to Christ and to reach their full potential as children of God.

Young people are looking for The Real Thing, and youth leaders who are totally dedicated can lead them to him.

An Effective Youth Leader Is Cooperative and Inspires Cooperation

If there is anything that inspires cooperation, it is a cooperative and helpful attitude. Others will support your efforts in direct proportion to the degree of support you give to them.

One of the great secrets of being a successful leader is to find out what people want, and help them get it. Remember: *People do things for their reasons — not yours!* When the people of your church and the youth in your group are achieving goals that are important to them, they will be supportive of your efforts.

There is no place in youth work for the person who always insists that things be done his or her way. A big part of successful work is flexibility — the ability to adjust to the needs and interests of others.

An Effective Youth Leader Is Organized

As a resource person, I have held seminars for youth workers all over the world. The most common complaint I hear from people who attend those seminars is, "I never seem to have enough time!"

Learning how to determine what you want to do and how to set up a plan to get it done is half the battle. Successful managers live by the motto, "Plan your work, and work your plan." They know it is a lot easier, safer and more pleasant to work when they know what they want to accomplish and have a definite plan for getting it accomplished. They also know that it is much easier to adjust for changes and emergencies when they have planned for them.

A youth leader who is organized can utilize his or her own strengths and abilities, and all the other resources available, to maximum advantage more often than can the person who just flies by the seat of the pants.

Are You a Winner?

In this chapter, I have given you some of the traits of the winners I have known in youth work. As you have read over them, have you said, "I wish I could be like that"? The fact is that you can!

Every one of the traits I have listed is a cultivated trait — not something that is inherited. Your effectiveness as a youth leader will be directly proportional to the extent to which you master each of them.

Remember, winners make their goals, losers make excuses. If youth work is important enough to you, you can become an effective youth leader.

You have a lot going for you! Your church wants you to be a success, the people in your youth group want you to be a success, the parents of the youngsters to whom you minister want you to succeed. Most of all, God wants you to succeed as an effective youth worker!

GROWTH EXERCISE

Rate yourself on a scale of 1 to 10 for each of the following traits of an effective youth leader:

1. *Enthusiasm*

2. *Positive mental attitude*

3. *Effective communicator*

4. *Loving person*

5. *Courage and integrity*

6. *Courtesy and consideration*

7. *Gratitude*

8. *Dedication*

9. *Cooperativeness and ability to inspire cooperation*

10. *Organizing ability*

Are you satisfied with your rating on each of the traits? If not, set a goal now for improving those weak areas.

Section II

Focus on Relationships

CHAPTER 4

Why Every Church Needs an Effective Youth Ministry

"Honey, there's something I've been wondering about," said a husband after many years of enjoying his wife's cooking.

"What's that, dear?" she asked.

"You always go to the supermarket and pick out a nice big ham; then you bring it home and cut it in half before you cook it. Why?"

"Well, that's what my mother always did," came the reply.

Curious, the man asked his mother-in-law the same question, "Why do you always cut the nice big ham in half before you cook it?"

"Well, that's what my mother always did," came the reply.

Now, because the man was taking on more of the cooking chores and wanted to learn, he followed through on his questioning. He asked the grandmother, "Why do you always cut the ham before you cook it?"

"It's simple, sonny," said the old lady. "I've never had a pot big enough to cook a whole one in!"

These days, virtually any church of some size has a youth ministry, but if you ask the members why, they will tell you something like, "Well, that's the way we've always done it!"

There Has to Be a Better Reason!

The fact of the matter is that many churches simply don't know why they invest as much money, time and talent in youth ministries as they do — they've just always done it! There has to be a better reason than that!

I seriously question whether a church can have an *effective* youth ministry without a clear understanding of why it is involved in such a program. The key word in that sentence is *effective*.

It is quite possible to have a youth ministry — even a youth ministry that attracts a lot of young people — without knowing why the church is doing it, or what that church wants to accomplish with its youth ministry.

Young people congregate at electronic game marts, pizza parlors, hamburger joints and theatres, but it takes a lot of imagination to call what happens in those places "ministry." Of course, attracting a crowd of young people is important, but if that's all that the youth ministry accomplishes, in my estimation it is a failure.

The purpose of this chapter is to help you focus on why an effective youth ministry is vital to the life of a church. It gets at the very heart of everything a church does, and centers on the relationship that church has with its youth.

Once we understand clearly why a church should have a good strong youth ministry, and what that youth ministry should accomplish for the church and for its young people, we will be in a better position to determine how a church should go about setting up and maintaining an effective youth ministry.

The first step in creating — or reshaping — a strong youth ministry is for enough people to become convinced that it is both necessary and possible.

Evaluation — the Key Questions

"Why should our church have a youth ministry?" That's the most vital question a church or its youth leaders can ask. Yet it is a question that few ever seriously ask.

Peter Drucker, who has been called "the father of American management," poses some serious questions for businesses and nonprofit organizations — including churches.

"What is our business?" he says is the most important question an organization can ask, both at its beginning and at every point of its growth. The fact that most churches consider the answer to that question so obvious as to need no answer, might very well explain why their youth ministries have so little impact on both the life of the church and the young people they are designed to serve.

"The business of our church is quite simple," youth ministers often say to me. "It is to preach the Gospel!"

"If that is so," I ask in response, "then why commit so many resources to buildings, to Sunday school literature, to a special youth ministry, to the various service ministries your church supports?

You see, there is more to being a church than simply preaching the Gospel, although that is a key element of a church's reason for existence. I should like to suggest some other considerations that are included in the business of running God's church in your community. Each of these has implications for the shape and direction of your youth ministry.

The business of the church includes (but may not be limited to):

- Bringing people into a vital relationship with the living Christ

- Creating an environment in which people can grow to full maturity in Christ

- Providing resources to assist people in their spiritual growth

- Assisting people in developing and maintaining the relationships that enrich their lives

- Guiding people in their efforts to make the Gospel relevant to their daily lives

- Having an impact on the moral/spiritual climate of the community

- Providing loving assistance to those in the community who need help

- Participating in the worldwide church's ministry to missions and service

- Maintaining the physical presence of Christ in the world

I could go on for many pages talking about important elements of the business of the church, but I think you get the point. The church exists as a vehicle through which people come to know, to serve and to grow to maturity in Christ.

All of that suggests that every church which has — or wants to have — at least one young person needs an active and effective youth ministry. It also suggests that the purpose of the youth ministry is to bring young people into a relationship with Christ, to nurture their growth to full maturity in him, and to enable them to realize their full potential as his creation.

My purpose here is not to define the business of your church for you. That is not my privilege or responsibility. My purpose is to help you to focus for yourself, and for all the people who have an impact on your youth ministry, why you want to have an effective youth ministry, and how that ministry should be conducted.

"If We Had No Youth Ministry . . . ?"

Another question that Professor Drucker raises for organizations to consider is this: "If we were not in this business, would we go into it?"

That question suggests that it is at best a waste of resources to pursue something as taxing as youth ministry simply because "it seems important." At worst, aimlessly wandering around holding youth activities robs your young people of the resources they need to become mature Christians and people.

To the question, "If we had no youth ministry, would we start one?" I hope your answer is a big, emphatic *yes!* But the next question that logically comes up is, "Why?" When you and your whole church can answer that question to your full satisfaction, you are well on your way to setting a strong course to a worthwhile goal, committing the necessary resources to get there, and developing an approach that results in a very effective youth ministry.

Five Reasons Every Church Needs an Effective Youth Ministry

Young People Have Special Needs, Desires and Interests

Adolescence is a time for growth, for learning, for experimenting.

Today's youth are active, alert, alive. They are attracted to action, to creativity, to each other. They want to be involved, stimulated, excited. Nothing is so big, so active, so dynamic as is the Gospel of Christ creatively presented.

I recently saw a teenaged friend in a hamburger joint, playing his guitar and singing songs he had written. Proudly, he told me that he would be singing in a nightclub at the beach the next summer. As we talked, he told me that he had never been invited to sing any of his compositions in the church he had attended all his life, although most of them were on religious themes. What a waste!

Patterns for life are being set for young people by the forces that surround them. They are bombarded constantly by television, radio, records, magazines, other young people and other voices that cry out for their attention. An effective youth ministry can help them to balance out the influences, to make sense of the endless questions they are asking, and to set directions that will lead them to a full and fruitful life as Christians.

Caring that young people have questions and needs is at least as important for a church as is offering answers and solutions.

Young People Are a Church's Investment in Its Future

Business people have long recognized that the growth and well-being of their companies is directly dependent on how good a job they do in developing their people to be leaders and good workers. Schools exist for the purpose of preparing people for future lives. Likewise, any church that diligently tries to "train up a child in the way he should go" is making a sound investment in its own future.

Financially, an effective youth ministry is a church's best investment in both its present and its future. Of course, buildings are important, but they only exist for the use of the people they serve.

Think how exciting it would be if, through a fruitful youth ministry, your church grows during the next 10 years to a point where the building you now have is entirely too small. At that point, all the resources you need would be available to build a larger facility.

Churches that consistently invest time, resources and money in active youth ministries find that the investment pays off in rich dividends.

Young People Have Much to Give to the Church Today

One big city church struggled for years with its need to double its parking space, its lack of space for youth activities, and vandalism committed by neighborhood children.

"Our only solution is to move to the suburbs and build a new church," some members argued. "We don't have the money. . . . Besides, our church needs to be right here," others said.

During Youth Week, the problem was given to a youth panel, which came up with the following suggestions: "Let's build a double-decker parking lot, put a basketball court on the top deck and ping pong and other activities on the lower level, and set up volunteer-staffed recreational programs to involve the children in the neighborhood."

Sure, there were problems with oil on the basketball court, balls that had to be stopped from going into the streets, and scheduling enough volunteers to help. But the parking problem resolved itself, the church saved a great deal of money, and the vandalism stopped almost immediately. As a bonus, the church found a new ministry.

There is a gold mine of resources in even a small group of young people whose ideas are sought, whose enthusiasm is channeled, and whose energies are utilized.

Children Matter a Great Deal to Parents Who Attend Church

Parents need all the help a church can give them in providing for the spiritual development of their children. Often parents feel that the church can offer their children constructive activities, training and opportunities to develop their talents that could never be provided by any other institution.

And parents want help. Families moving to new neighborhoods usually want to know about the schools, recreational facilities, hospitals and churches available for their children.

Christian Tradition Has Always Led in Compassionate Care of Children

In the first century, "inferior" or unwanted children were often left abandoned in pits or in the wilderness to die. Even Plato, the high-minded philosopher, advocated the practice as a way of making sure that only the strong would survive.

But Jesus said, "Suffer the little children to come unto me, and forbid them not . . . " The care and tenderness given children by the leaders and parents of the New Testament era became the model for the whole world.

Wasn't it the church that led the fight to rid our society of the sweatshops where children were forced to do adults' work? Hasn't the church led the way in setting up day-care centers for children of parents who must work?

Ministry to youth is a big part of the mission of a church.

Conclusion

An active and effective youth ministry is the best stewardship of the resources God has given to a church.

The story is told of a father who always told his son, "I don't have time," when the boy asked him to play. When the boy grew up and the father grew old, the father said, "Son, come sit awhile with me."

"Sorry, Dad, I don't have time," the boy replied.

Any church that provides well for the needs of its youth will find that its youth will provide well for its needs — now and for the years to come.

GROWTH EXERCISE

Write a brief answer to each of the following questions:

1. **Why should our church have an effective youth ministry?**

2. **What is the business of our church?**

3. **Who should be served by the youth ministry of our church?**

4. **If our church had no youth ministry, would we start one ? Why?**

5. **If I were not involved in youth work, would I go into it? Why?**

Once you have answered those questions to your satisfaction, it might be helpful to discuss them with someone else in your church.

CHAPTER 5

Understanding Young People

"If you think you understand teenagers, you're really confused!" read the sign in the office of one of the sharpest professional youth directors.

I found the sign both comforting and disturbing. It was comforting for me to know that I wasn't the only one baffled by the behavior of young people; but it was disturbing that a person who had had as much training and experience as he was still baffled by the behavior of adolescents.

"During the last three decades, young people have been analyzed, studied, generalized and criticized, but seldom understood," he said.

When asked why he thought teenagers were so hard to understand, he listed three big reasons:

- Teenagers are people. They can no more be lumped together than can adults, people of various races, or even politicians. They are individuals, with unique motivations, interests and fears.

- Young people seldom understand themselves and even more rarely can they adequately communicate what they do understand about themselves.

- Adolescents change so rapidly that they are different each time you see them. Their whole outlook on life can change within a matter of a few days.

"But as a professional youth director, you're expected to understand young people!" someone protested.

"No," he responded, "I don't get paid to understand them — *I get paid to be understanding toward them.*"

What a distinction! Understanding youth might be impossible, but as a youth leader, you can be understanding toward them. And there are some traits that can be seen to some extent in each of them.

Understanding young people is important not only from their point of view: the more you understand what makes them tick, the more you will be able to communicate with them, and the less frustrated you will be by their antics.

Basic Needs, Motivations and Drives of Youth

The Urge to Merge

Have you ever staged a retreat and noticed that no one signed up until one or two key young people said they were going? If so, you have experienced peer group pressure.

The need to be accepted by a certain group is probably the most powerful force you will encounter as you seek to minister to teenagers. In fact, psychologists and sociologists consistently list the desire to be accepted by peers as the need most commonly expressed by teenagers in their studies.

If you try to fight it, it can drive you bananas. However, if you understand it, it can be one of the most powerful tools you will have in your youth ministry.

A few years ago, the cry of youth in America was "Do your own thing!" The idea was that they would reject the traditions of adult society and seek to be "different." It soon became apparent that there was a set pattern to being "different."

Young people like to experiment, but more than that, they like to do what other young people are doing. This suggests several principles that will be important in your youth ministry.

- Provide for consistent and strong input from the young people you seek to serve.

- Allow young people to carry the ball as much as possible.

- Try to enlist the aid of key young people in making it easy for new people to break into your youth group.

- Stay alert for any sign that a person is being shoved out of the group.

Acceptance is often based on performance, and teenagers know that better than anyone. If they cannot perform or are not given the opportunity and encouragement in one group, they will probably seek to be accepted by another group.

Young people need to be allowed to do things and to be recognized for their accomplishments. Of course, some teenagers are more capable in certain areas than others, and the tendency is to keep going back to those who are capable and willing.

Regarding the matter of performance, there are some cautions:

- Watch out for the youngster who never says anything. He may be hurting inside and wishing he could get into things.

- Provide special recognition for the one who tries and fails. Having everyone laugh at him is probably a more traumatic experience than you will ever know.

- Don't believe the guy who says, "I don't care what anybody thinks about me." He cares!

- Make sure that great care is taken to adequately prepare young people for anything you want them to do.

Many a youth leader has turned a very destructive youngster into a model participant by asking for his or her help. The need to be needed is a very powerful force that can be used for the good of all the young people in your group.

Recently, I was asked to conduct a series of "rap sessions" with a very rowdy group of boys.

"What kind of feelings do you bring to this group meeting?" was my first question. After a few giggles, they started showing signs of being nervous.

"I'm scared!" one boy blurted out.

"What are you afraid of?" I asked.

"I'm scared you'll ask me to do something that will make me look dumb," he continued. A quick verbal trip around the room revealed that they were all afraid.

"You know what? I'm scared, too," I said. And it was the truth.

"C'mon, man! What are you scared of?" one of the boys asked cynically.

"I'm afraid that you guys will rip me up . . . that you will reject me," I replied.

Suddenly and dramatically, the tide turned. All at once they began trying to make me feel at home and a part of their group. When I confessed my fears and need to be needed by them, they responded with love. It was fantastic!

The idea that a youth director must remain strong and "have his stuff together" went out with the Dark Ages. You can only have a going youth group when the people in the group want it to happen, and the sooner you become human with them, the better.

Another major part of the "urge to merge" is reflected in the teenager's search for a mate. Second only to the need to feel accepted is the need for a deep personal relationship that could result in a lifelong union.

Try to buck it and you'll not only get clobbered, you will hurt a lot of young people in your group.

Junior-high and high-school students fall into love and out of it at a dizzying pace. Sometimes it is downright frustrating.

It sometimes shows up like this. You have a weekend retreat scheduled and Sally is in charge of the food. She calls you in tears and tells you that she and Bart have broken up. "If he's going, I'm staying home," she says.

You are tempted to brush it aside with a comment like, "Oh! That's silly!" or "You'll get over it." Better bite your tongue. Billy Graham once said, "I never make fun of puppy love because it is so serious to the puppies."

The youth director who meets the love crises with gentleness and kindness will become a valued friend of the people in his group.

Finally, the "urge to merge" poses problems for the teenager who has difficulty communicating. He may feel a lot of beautiful things for the group, but be totally unable to express those feelings.

Unfortunately, many teenagers lack the basic skills of communication. A youngster who stumbles over something you have asked him to read is likely to be laughed at by the group and is equally likely to react with hostility to their rejection.

Likewise, some of the people will be fantastically capable and outgoing communicators. They are likely to dominate every group discussion or activity. While the other members of the group may appear to admire them, those quieter ones may seethe with hostility but be unable to muster the courage to challenge them.

Facilitating the flow of communication among teenagers and between them and adults is a big part of the youth director's job.

The Emergence of Personal Identity

Much of the stormy nature of the teen years comes from fears about personal identity.

Finding his special place in the world is often a frightening search for an adolescent. Someone has described the situation as similar to a person setting sail on the ocean in hopes of finding the land of promise. He may want to turn back, and some do, but when he returns, he will find the scene has changed too much for him to feel comfortable.

A teenager stands in the no-man's land between childhood and adulthood, knowing that he or she must find a place in the adult world, but often very confused as to what it will be.

Through a process of experimentation, teens try to make some sense of all that is happening around them. Because they are afraid, they may attack the adult world as they perceive it. Of course, such attacks are usually met with counterattacks from the adults who feel the need to defend the world as they know it.

What the teenager needs most is a friend and guide — someone who knows something about both worlds. It is at this point that an understanding youth director can make a valuable contribution.

Fear is a constant companion for the typical teenager. He is afraid that he will be so different that he will not be acceptable. He may get caught up in worries over the size of his nose, the shape of his head, or the sound of his voice. Helping a person to accept himself, as he is, is one of the most valuable gifts you can offer.

Feelings of inferiority often plague teenagers in a church group. A girl may be afraid that what she has to offer will not be accepted as having value. She may worry a great deal about whether she will be considered attractive by boys.

It is sometimes amazing that adults react so negatively to the outward expressions of a sense of inferiority. Perhaps it is not so amazing, however, when one considers that many adults did not overcome basic feelings of inferiority themselves during their teen years.

It is indeed a gift of the Holy Spirit to be able to recognize the beauty in each person and to be able to seek out ways of affirming that beauty.

Another major category of fear is the *fear of failure.* A boy may stand up in front of the group and clown around, but just try to get him to take a serious part in a program and watch him run. Such a person is suffering from a fear of failure.

Teenagers often fear that they will fail at careers, at romance, at social acceptance, at almost anything they try. You can help a great deal by enouraging them to try new things and by standing with them whether they fail or succeed.

Although many teenagers would deny it, most of them suffer from a *fear of death or insanity*. They like horror stories and stories of people who have "gone off the deep end." To laugh about it all and to appear to take it lightly somehow seems to ease the pain of the fear they feel.

This kind of fear must be handled carefully. To ignore it is to desert the youngster at a time when he needs affirmation. To push him into a serious discussion before he is ready is to deepen the fear and to close off communication. Perhaps the key to success in this area is to be available, let him know you are available, but not be pushy.

Setting some limits on the experimentation is necessary, but these should be set carefully. As a youth director, you can be of great service to the church and its youth by helping them bridge the gap between what is accepted and what is desired. A principle that is always helpful is to always try to stimulate the flow of communication between the youngster and his church rather than serving as an interpreter to both.

Most of all, you can help in the emergence of personal identity by taking the people in your group seriously. As you are able to recognize their individuality and affirm its beauty, you will be able to assist them in their acceptance of themselves and others. As you learn to see each teenager as a person, you will be able to help them come to see themselves as worthwhile.

A Personal Faith in God

Another of the basic needs of any person is to establish a workable faith in God that will stand the test of time.

Someone has said that God does not have any grandchildren. Yet, in many groups the personal relationship with God is overlooked as a vital need of the youngster. In recent years there has been an awakening in the church that has brought this need to the forefront again.

It is not enough to assume that just because a young person attends all the activities, has Christian parents and says all the right words, he or she has forged a personal relationship with God. "She was always a good girl until . . . " is a fairly typical expression.

The reality it reveals is that somewhere down the line, "she" failed to establish a faith that worked for her. The misconceptions that plague most teenagers in their ideas about God are sometimes overwhelming.

"What's your greatest fear?" a friend once asked a young man who was one of the top studio musicians in Nashville, Tennessee.

"Well, I have to fly a lot," he said, "and I'm always afraid that the plane is going to crash."

"Oh! You are afraid of dying?" my friend asked.

"No! What I am afraid of is having to stand before God and face him," he replied. "I try real hard to be good, but it's so difficult for me."

It was pretty obvious that with all his success he still saw himself as a terrible person and saw God as an owl-eyed monster sitting on a hill watching his every move. He was sure that sooner or later he was going to get hit with a lightning bolt.

He needed someone to share with him the reality that God loves him and wants the best for him. As that realization becomes focused in his life, he can become an exciting and excited Christian.

Much of the restlessness of teenagers can be attributed to the fact that they are empty inside. The tendency is to try to find fulfillment in everything but God. So how do you as a youth director help young people establish a meaningful relationship with God?

First, leave the preaching to the pastor. Sure, you can share your personal faith in God and explore questions about God, but they expect the pastor to preach — not you.

Second, seek to help them focus the questions about their personal ideas about God and their own lives.

Third, don't back away from your church's stand on the issues of sin and guilt. Your efforts to make it easy for them may give them a distorted view. They need to come to recognize their own need for God.

Fourth, help them explore their rightful place in the universe — to come to know that each has a place in the universe, but that none is at its center.

Finally, help them come to see God as the reason for living — something to live for.

Opportunities to Grow and Learn

This need is very basic to the teenager and it provides your greatest opportunity to shine and show your creative genius.

But watch it! Your creative genius may become a liability rather than an asset. A youth director who is too good at too many things tends to stifle growth rather than encourage it. I have talked about the fear of failure that is so prevalent among teenagers. If you become known as a whiz at music and art and a host of other things, the youth in your charge become too timid to try these things for themselves.

Since young people learn best by doing, a helpful principle is to never do anything for them that they can do for themselves. They might not do it as well as you could, but there is value in trying.

It is really tough to watch youngsters slop over a sign advertising a forthcoming event when you know you could have done it well. Give them a chance to try, and if they fail, give some guidance. Eventually they may be able to do a surprisingly good job. If so, you have not only gotten rid of a job, you have found a talent. More importantly, you will have helped them discover their capabilities.

Another principle that is helpful is to cultivate a sense of responsibility among your teenagers without expecting them to always act responsibly. Responsibility has to be learned — it does not come automatically for most people.

Sometimes the pressures of a youth director's job are such that the emphasis is on the quality of the event rather than on what the young people gain from it. When the success of a retreat, for example, is more important than the needs of the young people who attend, something is out of focus.

Discipline provides another one of those opportunities to grow and learn. The ultimate goal of controlling behavior is to create a sense of self-control within the young people themselves.

To be sure, the rights of others must be protected, and you should have no hesitancy to do that. However, if that is all that ever comes out of discipline, the opportunity for growth has been missed.

The Need to Have Fun

To be effective, your efforts at youth ministry must take into account the fundamental need of young people to have fun.

The business of learning about God can be a thrilling and exciting experience. Anybody who says that God does not have a sense of humor has never taken a good look at a monkey or a duckbilled platypus. A study of Jesus' life shows that the only two times he ever went to great lengths to explain his behavior were to explain why he and his disciples were so joyful. Even on the night before he was crucified, he talked to his disciples about joy.

As a youth director, you will be miles ahead if you can come to see, and help your church to see, that young people are going to have fun.

Play is, for young people, the equivalent of work among adults. The silly giggles, the endless picking and the good-natured clowning can be seen as a nuisance or as the natural expression of the boundless energy and zest for living possessed by the young. Try to block it, and you and they will stay frustrated. Learn to channel it and work around it — even to share it with them — and you will become indispensible to them.

If you accept this premise, it then becomes your task to structure activities that flow with this drive and that provide enough release from pressures that the youth welcome the opportunity to go to church.

The Sex Drive

If there is any place that young people should learn about the sex drive, it is at church.

It is not enough to simply say, *"Don't!"* We must seek to help them see themselves as total beings created by God. And sexuality is a part of that totality.

I talked earlier about some of the fears that plague teenagers, but none is greater than the fear that they will not be normal sexually. Teens will joke about this fear, deny it, and otherwise try to cover up for it.

Sex is such an exploited subject in almost every area of our society that the church dare not remain silent on the subject.

But watch out! This is an explosive issue within the local church. This is one of those areas in which you need to work hard to make sure that you are reflecting the values taught by your church. You need a lot of help by the pastor and the other leaders of your church in establishing a worthwhile and workable system of communicating about sex.

The Need to Establish Goals and Values

There are some big questions that face young people as they come to adulthood. Perhaps none is as important as the question of how they will spend their lives and what values will guide them for the future.

Unfortunately, this is all too often left to chance. Thus, many young people come to adulthood with no clear understanding as to why they do the things they do, and values are soon forgotten. Worse still is the situation in which a person sees God as only casually interested in his life and who sets a course for the future on the basis of purely a secular view of human beings.

Young people are being bombarded at school with questions about the values of society; they are practically brainwashed by television and radio to adopt certain lifestyles; and they are under constant pressure to conform to some code of conduct.

It is very important that you constantly seek ways to focus goals and values for your teenagers. That focus should always be consistent with the Bible and your church's understanding of what the Bible is saying to us today.

"Let them alone! Let them make up their own minds," the humanists say. That might work if the humanists, too, would let teens alone. But they won't. In school and through the communications media, teens are hit with everything from humanism to outright atheism. And at the same time, they are denied any teaching on the Bible and the privilege of prayer.

In adolescence, people are deciding how they will spend their lives. It is crucial that they come to understand that God has something to say about that decision.

Conclusion

It is perhaps not as important to understand young people as it is to be understanding toward them and to have a basic grasp of the needs, motivations and drives that make them do the things they do. When your ministry to youth is primarily aimed at meeting their needs, you will be able to make a valuable contribution to their lives.

GROWTH EXERCISE

As you review each of the basic needs, motivations and drives we have discussed, think of some person who helped you deal with those feelings when you were a teenager. Write a brief description of how that person helped you cope.

CHAPTER 6

Counseling Youth

One of the most important roles you will ever play as a youth leader can loosely be called counseling young people. I say "loosely called" because few youth directors have either the training or the client-counselor relationship that can qualify them as professional counselors.

But to the extent that you view counseling as assisting a youngster over life's rough spots; providing a solid sounding board on which that youngster can talk out problems; and providing an understanding and caring attitude to troubled young people, you can be an effective counselor.

Studies have shown that the assistance young people receive from caring youth leaders can be a very valuable aid in sorting through the complexities of their lives. The quiet talks after a meeting, the long "raps" on retreats, and even the formal sessions with youngsters and/or their parents can all be very productive.

Of course, the subject of counseling young people is far too broad to be covered adequately in one chapter of a book; however, there are some basic points that can help you in guiding the young people who come to you for help.

Recognizing Counseling Opportunities

Why is it that some leaders seem to do a lot of counseling, while others seem to do almost none? Asked another way, why do young people seek out one youth leader, but feel reluctant to talk to another?

Here are several factors that enter into it. They offer clues as to how to open the door for young people to come to you for assistance.

Be Approachable

Openness is the key to having young people eager to talk out their problems with you. A young person with a real problem might feel very cautious about approaching an adult to talk about that problem.

From the youngster's point of view, there are several real risks:

- The youth leader might laugh off the problem and say, "Oh, don't take it so seriously." Regardless of the adult's intentions, such a brush-off feels like rejection to a teenager. The problem may seem trivial to you, but to the young person, it is important at the time.

- The adult might condemn the young person for having such feelings, or for engaging in the behavior that brought on the problem. Again, a judgmental response feels like rejection. As a youth leader, your most productive posture is total nonjudgmental acceptance of anyone who comes to you to talk about a problem or concern.

- The youth leader might betray the confidence of a young person who comes for help. Absolute confidentiality is so vital that I will have more to say about it later in this chapter.

- The youth leader might prescribe a course of action — as what he sees as the only viable option — that the young person knows he or she cannot pursue. In other words, an adult approached for help in making a decision might very well try to take charge of the person's life.

Regardless of how insignificant you might feel that some of these fears are, they stand as barriers between you and young people you could — and would like to — help through counseling.

Here are some tips that can help you establish a reputation as approachable:

1. *Verbally express a willingness to talk privately* with any of the young people.

2. *Make yourself readily available* to talk.

3. *Treat each person in the group with dignity and respect.* Never join in the ribbing of a member of the group when to do so could damage a delicate set of feelings.

4. *Keep public criticism to an absolute minimum.*

5. *Always take seriously any concerns* that young people express to you.

Stay Alert for Signals

A few young people will simply approach you and blurt out, "I want to talk with you about a problem." Very often, the approach is much more subtle.

Here are some signals to watch for:

1. ***Hanging around:*** A youngster who is experiencing some difficulty might simply start hanging around where you are. He or she may simply be lonely, wanting someone to talk with. That in itself is a problem that should be taken seriously, but it might well be a symptom of a much deeper problem.

   When a young person lingers in your presence, by all means take the time to engage that person in conversation, and provide an opportunity for him or her to open up.

2. ***Disruptive actions:*** Many youth directors blow a valuable opportunity to minister to a deeply troubled young person simply by assuming the role of disciplinarian. To kick a young person out of a group session or become angry and strike out at some teenager who is disrupting the whole process could close a door that needs desperately to be left open.

   When a youngster is disruptive, always find out what is behind the disruptive behavior.

3. ***Prolonged absence:*** When a young person who attends regularly suddenly drops out for two or three weeks, usually you can be sure that there is something traumatic going on in that person's life. If you can get to the person during that time, you might be able to change the course of his or her life.

   Some youth directors feel that to go after members of the group who drop out is to chase after them, and to come across as overly solicitous. Of course, you can spend all your time chasing people who don't show up when they're expected. However, expressing concern for an individual who has been an active part of the group and suddenly drops out hardly seems solicitous to me.

4. ***Withdrawal from the group:*** When a young person feels like an outsider, he might withdraw from the group and say nothing. Not all people who feel rejected

become aggressive. Often they refuse to participate in the activities going on — even though they are forced by their parents to attend. Any youngster who is outside the circle of your church group needs your personal touch.

Usually you can bet that the church group is not the only arena from which such a person withdraws. Enough withdrawal can lead to some very serious personal problems.

Deal with Problems Early

Most problems that show up in the symptoms listed above simply won't go away if left alone. A person who suffers from chronic loneliness, from disruptive attitudes or from an unwillingness to risk rejection, needs help.

Personal problems have a way of compounding themselves if they continue to exist for very long. When a person experiences a hurt, the natural response is for emotional scar tissue to form around the injury. The more hurts one experiences, the more layers of scar tissue that develop. Finally, the person becomes unreachable.

Most professional counselors agree that the earlier a problem is detected and dealt with effectively, the better the chances of a complete recovery.

Be an Active Listener

Sensitivity to the feelings expressed by words or actions is an art that requires a great deal of practice. What a young person doesn't say is often more important than what the person says. In fact, a teenager might be feeling precisely the opposite of what gets expressed in a heated discussion.

For example, a young person who suddenly blurts out, "I hate you!" in a group meeting is most likely feeling something like this: "I love you, and want desperately for you to accept me, but I feel rejected. That hurts!"

To say to such a person, "Aw, come on, don't act that way," not only fails to get at the real problem, it can compound the damage.

I will have much more to say about the techniques of active listening in the chapter on "How to Communicate Effectively with Young People." Suffice it to say at this point that listening and observing are two of the most important ways of recognizing counseling opportunities.

How to Open the Door
for Counseling

Just as it is often difficult for young people who need counseling to approach you, it is sometimes difficult for you to approach someone who needs help. Approach abruptly, and you may offend or frighten off the person; approach too subtly, and the person may not pick up on your signal.

So how do you go about opening that all-important door? Here are some guidelines I've found helpful:

1. *Never sneak up on a young person.* Occasionally parents will call you and say something like this: "I'm having a real problem with Mary. ... I wish you could talk to her for me — but don't let her know that I called you!"

   Most professional counselors agree that honesty is a necessary ingredient for a successful counseling arrangement. If you must start out with a deception, it's like having two strikes against you from the beginning.

   There's another problem with the sneaky approach. Usually, what the parent describes as a "problem with Mary" involves a breakdown in communication within the family. If you try to intervene without involving the whole family, you will likely get caught in the middle — between the parents and child. As a result, you won't be able to help much in solving deeper problems.

   A third problem with the sneaky approach is that by agreeing to "talk with Mary," you assume responsibility for solving the problem. If anything productive can be done, it can only be done while the problem remains the concern of the affected parties.

2. *Never accuse or attack.* "You've been pretty uncooperative lately; is there something bothering you?" is a rather judgmental approach to attempting to open a door for counseling.

   When you accuse a person of some unsatisfactory behavior or attack the friends he is running around with, you automatically put him on the defensive.

A far more productive approach is to say something like, "I feel our relationship isn't as good as I'd like it to be. . . . You matter a lot to me! Could we talk about it?"

By focusing the attention on your relationship with the young person, you can indicate an interest. To do so is to come across more as a friend than as a judge who has found the person guilty. And few people will be offended by an invitation to deepen a relationship.

3. *Always express caring concern.* "I know there have been a lot of painful changes occurring in your life lately, and I'd really like you to know that I care. . . . Would you like to talk about how some of those changes have affected you?" is a better approach than, "Boy, you look down! You'd better unload on somebody!"

Fear of rejection, feelings of isolation and hopelessness can be overcome by a genuine show of caring concern by an adult. Before a young person will risk exposing the real feelings and fears that lie deep inside, three things must be present:

- First, there must be the feeling that talking to an adult is safe.
- Second, there must be the hope that something good can come from the effort.
- Third, significant contact must be established.

Those things can best occur when you as a youth leader express your love and concern for the young person.

4. *Always be gentle but forthright in your approach.* Some youth leaders are so vague in their attempts to help that the young people they reach out to touch cannot figure out what they are trying to say to them.

Inviting a youngster over "for a Coke" so you can drop a bombshell is seldom productive, and can sometimes backfire on you. Most young people appreciate a gentle but forthright approach. They might not be ready to talk about the problem; they might not even perceive what you see as being a problem. But they will respect your openness and honesty.

5. *Invite, don't push; suggest, don't demand.* One of the most common complaints of young people about

youth leaders is that they are preachy.

Since one of the struggles young people must go through is finding their own identity, they can be very independent. Sometimes they just want to be left alone. Adults, however well-meaning they may be, are often barred from the decision-making process of a teenager's life. It is very painful to watch a young person continue to struggle with a problem, or follow the terrible advice he receives from peers, but he must be given the freedom to make choices.

All you can really do is invite the person to talk about the problem you see, and suggest that there might be alternatives that have not yet been explored. But in the final analysis, it is best to respect each person's privacy.

6. *Remember whose problem it is.* Taking the problems of others on their own shoulders is a tendency among adults who seek to become youth leaders. Unfortunately, most of us have difficulty handling our own problems.

But there is an even larger issue to be considered here. When we assume responsibility for another person's problem, we deny him the opportunity to get in touch with his own coping resources.

I have found the "monkey-on-the-back theory" very useful in this regard. It works like this: When a person tells you about a problem and asks, "What should I do?" that person is attempting to put the monkey on your back. If you say, "Well, if I were you . . . " you are accepting the monkey. The theory is this: "A smart monkey doesn't monkey with another monkey's monkey."

Effective youth leaders learn to help other people discover their own resources for coping with life's rough spots.

7. *Try to give hope, but don't promise quickie solutions.* "Give it some time — you'll get over it!" might express what you feel about the jilting of a broken-hearted "puppy lover," but it's not likely to be very helpful or convince the person you know how deeply he or she is hurt.

Few problems can be worked out in 30 minutes or an hour — despite the impression created by happy endings on television. Pain and struggle are a very real part of life, and you can be most productive by helping young people develop ways of coping with them.

One phrase Christian counselors often use is, "Just turn the problem over to the Lord," or "Just pray about it." Most people find that this is much easier for someone else to say than it is for them to do. Of course God is available to help us cope with life's problems, and ultimately, drawing on his resources is the greatest source for finding solutions, but the task of counseling involves much more than telling someone to "pray about it." Helping a young person *learn how* to draw on God's resources in times of crisis is not only useful for a particular situation, it gives them a coping mechanism that will be useful to them for the remainder of their lives.

As a Christian youth worker, you have the privilege of enabling young people to discover all of the resources within themselves and the infinite resources of a loving God. Those resources cannot be discovered instantly or easily. It takes time, and it takes guidance from a person who has found those resources and is willing to guide another in discovering them.

Confidentiality — Absolute

The cardinal sin in counseling is to reveal confidential discussions. It is absolutely crucial for any counselor who works with young people to maintain a reputation as one who can be trusted.

Very often after you have counseled young people, you will be approached by their parents and asked to give them information about what you discussed. "We have a right to know," they will say. It is a valid argument, but the other side of that coin is this: if a youngster knows that you tell his parents what was told to you in confidence, he will not trust you and will tell you only what he wants the parents to find out. Most parents understand this when you tell them that your desire is to be genuinely helpful and ask for their support in making it possible for you to maintain the contact necessary to remain helpful.

Word spreads like wildfire among teenagers, and if one of the group feels his confidence has been violated, you can be sure that others in the group will know about it quickly. Soon others will talk with you only superficially.

Also, great care should be exercised in bringing to the attention of the group, even in a request for prayer, any information you have received in counseling. If you feel the prayers of the group would be valuable, ask the person involved to bring the problem to the attention of the group, or at least ask the person for permission to bring the matter to the group.

To make sure that you are covered with the other young people in the group, it is a good idea to state in advance, "I have asked Sue if it would be all right for me to bring this to your attention for prayer, and she has said she would like for me to do that."

Counseling Techniques

In counseling young people, a casual, comfortable kind of atmosphere is best. The front seat of an automobile, or sitting on a floor or in comfortable chairs is a suitable setting for a counseling situation. It is extremely difficult to communicate across a desk because of the authority a desk symbolizes.

Listen to the Problem

After a minimum of casual talk, lead the person to state succinctly for you the problem as he perceives it. This is a crucial step.

You may have already identified in your own mind where the problem lies — rightly or wrongly — but the fact is that the person who comes for help always has some perception of his own as to what the problem is. If you are to be helpful, you must understand how he perceives the problem.

Allow the person to talk out all feelings concerning that problem by telling you just what he sees the problem to be, how he feels about it and the dilemma it poses.

Once you have listened to the person's assessment of the problem, it is often helpful to express loving concern for the pain it causes. In fact, often the most valuable thing to come out of a counseling situation is the comfort that comes from having someone care that the person has a problem.

The need as expressed may seem trivial to you, but if it is important enough for the person to discuss with you, it is important enough for you to take seriously.

Teenagers want to be taken seriously. As an adult, you may be well aware that the youthful struggles of infatuation are quite temporary, but to the young person whose heart is broken, the end of a romance is a tragedy. Whatever the situation may be, it is important to let the young person know that you take him seriously as an individual.

Get a Contract

Once you have listened carefully to the person's assessment of the problem, then ask, "What can I do to help?" It is important that you find out what the person is expecting from you.

Very often you will find that the person's expectations of you are totally unrealistic. It is better to be honest and simply say, "I cannot do that," than to allow the person to believe you are capable of something you are not.

"If my daddy would just get off my back, everything would be all right," might be a young person's assessment of the problem. "Why don't you talk to him and see if you can get him off my back?" It just may be that talking to the father is not the solution to the problem at all. Certainly, your agreeing to go and straighten out another person is not much of a solution.

It is equally important that you let the person know your expectations of him. Many people who will come to you for counseling will expect you to do everything for them. That simply is not possible, and it is undesirable for you to assume their responsibilities.

Caring and sharing in a person's pain is one thing, but trying to bear the pain for them is an entirely different matter.

Assess the Real Problem

"Here are some things you might want to take a look at," is a very helpful way of focusing on factors that are present in the person's life which did not come out in his description of the problem. While it is true that you do not have all the answers, any person who comes to you for counseling will quite likely weigh your suggestions very seriously. If you believe there is something deeper involved than was stated, try to bring it into focus in a way that is not threatening or offensive.

Ask the Holy Spirit for guidance in trying to determine for yourself the root cause of the problem being brought to your attention.

Explore Alternatives

Once you have listened to the person's assessment of the problem, cleared the air as to what you can and cannot do, and assessed the problem from a deeper level, you can then help the person to explore all the alternatives that are available.

Very often people who are experiencing difficulty have narrowed things down to a point that they feel there are no options and that the inevitable is going to happen. It is helpful for people to see that there are options and that they can affect the situation by their actions. By helping them to explore the alternatives, you give them hope that they can change the situation, and you also suggest that they have a responsibility to do something on their own to bring about change.

Allow the Person to Choose

Once the alternatives have been explored, you can transfer the responsibility for the decision to the person you are counseling. I cannot overemphasize how important it is that the person make the choice.

Assure him that you will be his friend no matter what comes from the decision. If he chooses an alternative which is unacceptable to you, make it clear that regardless of what the decision is, you are going to be loving and receptive if he comes to you again. It is very helpful to avoid the impression that if the person comes back to you, you might say, "See, I told you so."

God respects a person's freedom of choice, and we as Christian workers must do the same thing. It is pretty obvious that God does not like all the choices that we make, but he allows us the freedom to make those destructive choices. And no matter what we do, he is always standing with open arms ready to receive us. Can we do less for the people to whom we minister in his name?

Close with Prayer

It is a good idea to close every counseling session with prayer if the person you are counseling is willing. If he joins you in prayer, it usually helps to reinforce the decision he has made.

In fact, when you are counseling a Christian, you might be able to tell when the counseling has been effective by the person's willingness to pray and turn the situation over to God.

Some people shy away from the idea of praying with a person who comes for counseling, but as Christian workers, we have the high privilege of talking to God in behalf of those who feel the need.

It is also important, once the person leaves, that you engage in regular intercessory prayer in his behalf. As a Christian you have available the full redemptive power of Jesus Christ to work in your friends' lives. Take full advantage of it.

Follow Up

Once the counseling session is complete, it is important that you set up a follow-up reporting mechanism. You may want to simply say, "Give me a call and let me know how you come out," or you may want to set up another meeting.

If some outside help is needed, it might be helpful at this point to arrange for it.

The value of reinforcing through follow-up what has been done in counseling cannot be overemphasized. One valid reinforcement is to have the person who has worked through a problem share it with the whole group and rejoice with his friends over the victory through Jesus Christ.

When, How and to Whom to Refer

Many youth leaders don't feel really qualified to counsel young people, and tend to refer them to professionals. Unfortunately, many of the secular counselors available are openly atheistic, and some are even zealous about "knocking down religious superstitions."

In *The Doctor and the Soul,* Victor Frankl, an Austrian psychiatrist, makes the bold statement, "Many persons being seen by the doctor ought to be seen by their priest." You may not be a priest, but the implication is clear — a very high percentage of the personal difficulties church young people and their parents experience are basically spiritual problems.

When a young person comes to someone he has identified as a spiritual leader and asks questions that deal with deep personal conflicts, to simply pack him off to an atheistic counselor is to abdicate the responsibility for nurturing spiritual and personal development.

However, there will be times when you realize you are in over your head, and that the problem before you requires attention from someone with more training and experience than you have. Knowing how to recognize those times and what to do when you encounter them is an important part of being a youth leader.

When to Refer

Here are some pointers that can help you determine when to refer:

1. ***When the person is seriously depressed (inordinately sad) over an extended period of time, it is a good idea to call for professional help.*** Now, all young people go through "down times" when they feel the cards in the game of life are stacked against them. But when the depression lasts more than a few weeks, seems to have no basis in circumstances, affects the person's eating habits, or impairs the person's ability to function as a part of a group, there is usually a serious problem. When any of these symptoms appear, it is a good idea to discuss the problem with someone who has some special training in dealing with depression.

2. ***Anytime a young person speaks (even casually) about suicide, it is a good idea to ask for help.*** Most people who talk about suicide or even threaten suicide don't take their own lives, but it is almost impossible for even the professionals to predict which ones of them will follow through with the act of suicide. Remember, the National Institute of Mental Health reports that the third leading cause of death among teenagers is suicide — ranking only behind accidental deaths and violent deaths, and above all natural causes of death. A good rule to follow is: *Always take a suicide threat seriously.*

3. ***When there is a strong indication of any serious involvement with drugs or alcohol, seek outside help.*** Of course, young people are increasingly experimenting with smoking pot, and drinking an occasional beer is becoming widespread. However, the incidence of drug addiction and alcoholism among teenagers is becoming alarmingly prevalent. If you feel that chemical dependency is impairing a person's ability to function, by all means attempt to get him some professional help.

4. ***Excessive withdrawal is another significant signal that a person is losing touch with reality.*** Some people are naturally shy and tend to keep their distance from groups, but a person who is seriously withdrawn could have real problems — both internally and in forming relationships.

5. ***Watch for any sudden and extreme change in behavior patterns.*** For example, if you notice that a person who has been outgoing and talkative suddenly becomes withdrawn and quiet, keep an eye on him to see if the new pattern persists. If it does, suggest professional help.

6. ***Watch for compulsive behavior or self-fulfilling prophecies.*** A person who constantly says, "I knew I couldn't do it! I always fail!" could only be lacking self-confidence, but such a person could have serious personal identity problems. Try to inspire self-confidence by enabling him to do small tasks, moving on to greater tasks. If the pattern persists, suggest he seek help.

How and to Whom to Refer

Some youth leaders and many parents are quite unrealistic in their expectations of professional counselors. It is easy to think that all that must happen is that the person be dragged into the presence of a trained counselor and the problem will go away. Unfortunately, it almost never happens.

Here are some referral techniques that can assist both the professional and the person referred in making the most of the counseling situation:

1. ***Refer, don't abandon!*** Often the counselor must be objective — even detached — in dealing with the person. The person struggling through a deep problem needs a great deal of support from loving adults and other young people.

2. ***Involve your minister!*** Unless your minister tells you otherwise, he or she should always be the first person with whom you discuss a serious problem — before you refer the young person to anyone for counseling.

3. ***Insist the person initiate the counseling request!*** Most professional counselors and organizations insist that the person needing counseling set up his or her own appointments. The reason is quite simple: unless the person who is to be counseled wants help badly enough to ask for it, there is little hope for success. You can't solve another person's problems; you can only assist that person in finding his or her own solutions.

4. *Try to get the parents involved!* Usually when a young person is having problems, those problems (or at least their solutions) involve the parents. When a family approaches a counselor and says, *"We* have a problem, and *we* want to work on it *together,"* the counselor can be much more productive in dealing with the problem.

5. *Don't build up false hopes for instant solutions!* Most serious problems take months to work through — even if all goes well. Some even take years, and a few may never be completely solved. The idea that a person can "go to a 'shrink' and get his head straightened out in a couple of visits" is totally unrealistic. Most problems developed over a long period of time, and they will need a lot of caring concern over a long period of time to be worked out.

6. *Always follow up!* When you refer a person for help and he fails to stick with the counseling program, the result can be a worse situation than existed before help was offered. "I tried that, and it didn't work!" such a person might say to anyone who tries to help in the future. Follow through to see that the counseling program is helping, that the counselor is being helpful, and that the desired improvement is actually becoming reality.

7. *Support through daily prayer!* The tendency is to say, "Well, all I can do now is pray." That is a lot more than you might realize. The Christian church has always maintained that prayer gets results. Sincere and continuous prayer might very well be the most powerful force at work in a troubled person's life. It is not a last resort for a helpless youth leader, but a necessary function of a loving adult.

8. *Know the counselor to whom you refer!* Just as there are differences among doctors, lawyers and ministers, there are differences among counselors. Educational criteria, professional standards and limits on counseling practices vary widely from state to state — some states have none. Make sure that the person to whom you refer a young person is professionally competent and motivated by concern.

Perhaps of even greater concern to a church youth leader is the fact that some counselors are openly antagonistic toward anything "religious." To refer a young person who is already having problems to an anti-Christian counselor is like throwing a lamb into a den of wolves.

You owe it to the young people within your group to cultivate a good working relationship with qualified Christian counselors in your area who will work with you — not against you — in your efforts to assist troubled people.

GROWTH EXERCISE

There are two parts to this exercise. Depending on your present situation, either or both of them could be useful to you:

Part 1: *As you review the chapter, think of someone who was helpful to you at some point in your life by using some of the techniques we have discussed. Also, think of people who could have been more helpful if they had used some of those techniques. Make notes on how you will use some of those ideas in dealing with some of the young people you encounter.*

Part 2: *Make a survey of the area counseling resources available to young people and parents. Give special attention to listing qualified Christian counselors you might call upon for help. Keep the list handy for future reference.*

CHAPTER 7

How to Communicate Effectively with Young People

*A guy and a girl are walking down a beach on a beautiful moon-
lit night. They pause for a moment, and he turns to her, takes her
hand into his hands, and softly speaks to her. "I love you!" he says.*

"I love you, too!" she replies.

"Will you marry me?" he asks.

"Yes!" she answers.

They kiss, and walk slowly on down the beach.

My friend, that is effective communication! With a few carefully chosen actions, and 12 small words, the lives of two people are
significantly changed forever.

By comparison, most of our efforts to communicate with young
people fall far short of that brief interchange between our two
romantic characters. Of course, few of us ever are influenced by
the motivational factors that set the stage for that excellent bit of
communication, but the fact is that most of us could communicate
much more effectively with young people than we do.

To get a better handle on how to communicate effectively
with young people, it might be helpful to look at exactly what
happened in the interchange between the two lovers:

First, there was the sending of messages. They each conveyed
precisely what they wanted to convey to the other. *Second,* there
was a receiving of messages. They each received the meaning
behind the messages sent by the other. *Third,* the messages produced
the desired response.

Simply stated, effective communication is: *the right person
saying the right thing, in the right way, to the right people, at the
right time and in the right place to produce the desired response.*

Thus, the purpose of all attempts to communicate is to convey
a message; the objective of all efforts at communicating is to have our
messages received and understood; and the goal of all communication

is to produce a desired response.

But there are factors which keep our communication attempts from being effective. Usually they fall into two categories: interference and poor communication techniques. To help us understand how those factors work against us in our efforts to communicate effectively with young people, and to overcome them, I have divided this chapter into three subject areas:

- Why is it so hard to reach young people today?

- Communication through the basic needs of young people

- Tested and proven communication techniques

Why Is It So Hard to Reach Young People Today?

Anyone who is handed the responsibility of communicating with young people today soon learns that it is a tough assignment. "Kids today are not that different from when we were growing up" is a common attitude among adults. However, anyone dealing with those kids must confront the fact that it is a tougher job than at any other period of the church's history.

Collision with the Future

"In the two short decades between now and the twenty-first century, millions of ordinary, psychologically sound people will face an abrupt collision with the future." That prediction was made in 1970 by Professor Alvin Toffler in a book called *Future Shock*. Professor Toffler's prediction has already come to pass. "Future shock is the dizzying disorientation brought on by the premature arrival of the future," he said. "Change is avalanching upon our heads, and most people are grotesquely unprepared to cope with it."

It is not simply the changes themselves but the rate at which change occurs now that is so disorienting and which makes permanence a thing of the past. Professor Toffler observes that millions of young people are so ignorant of the past that they think the present is normal.

To get a focus on just how dramatic this rate of change is, it might be helpful for your youth group members to make a list of all the things and services of which they avail themselves in the normal course of daily life. Once an exhaustive list is prepared, go through and mark off those things and services which were not available prior to the end of World War II. It is rather shocking to observe that almost everything we encounter right now, at least in its present form, is a product of this lifetime.

One out of every five Americans changes his place of residence each year, according to the latest report of the U.S. Census Bureau. These people are transferred by their employers, go looking for work in other cities, and more and more are on the move simply trying to find themselves.

Connectedness

Another major factor is summed up in Marshall MacCluhan's concept of "the global village." Mr. MacCluhan observes that through the communications media, everything is so instantaneous that the world has shrunk in size to become one great big village. The big problem is that while we have the electronic capability of communicating instantly with millions of people around the world, we are not yet ready to face up to becoming a unified world.

The teenagers in your church are more likely to be aware of what is happening among teens in New York and California than what is happening with the other young people in your youth group.

Information is being sent out so fast and in such volumes that it is difficult for the typical person to keep up with what is going on around him. The process of selection makes it necessary for certain bits of information to be filtered out. Much of what gets filtered out as irrelevant, or useless information, is what you are working hardest to convey.

An interesting thing happened on our journey to the global village. In order to keep up with the hectic pace, to make it in the world of business, and to take advantage of all that technology had to offer us, adults became separated from their children. Perhaps *separated* is not a strong enough word — maybe the word *isolated* fits better.

Children were segregated into schools, scout troops, YMCA groups, boys' clubs, athletic leagues — the list is endless. All of this isolation has forced young people to make it with their peers in order to survive. The result is that they are much more concerned about what other young people are saying and doing than they are about any message they might receive from the church.

Affluence and Mobility

Another major obstacle in communicating with young people today might be described as the combination of affluence and mobility.

America is the richest nation in the history of the world. We try to do everything better than anybody else. There seems to be a preoccupation with bigness. There is big business, big government and massive education.

But with all that we have provided, there is great dissatisfaction and the fear that we are being overwhelmed by our own systems. Newspapers recently told the story of a girl who, on her 21st birthday, found a thousand-dollar bill wrapped around each of the 21 candles on her cake. One week later the girl killed herself and left her parents this note: "You have given me everything to live with and nothing to live for."

The automobile industry, the electronics industry and the entertainment industries have made this the world's most entertained generation ever. "We've got more to do in this country than any other country in the world," a well-known television commercial says. With an ignition key, the typical middle-class teenager has entree to everything from mass-produced hamburgers and pizzas to giant bowling alleys, miniature golf and movies. Despite the presence of transistor radios, stereo sets, video games and what seems like nonstop television, however, many kids are simply bored.

We have declared war on illiteracy, and although far too many people are still illiterate, this is the best-educated generation the world has ever produced. Yet some schools are so violent that teachers' unions are demanding the presence of security guards. In some states, teachers are even carrying firearms to protect themselves from the students.

All this bigness has a certain depersonalizing, and in some cases dehumanizing, effect upon the young as well as the old in our society. It is very difficult now for people to really get in touch with one another.

Disintegration

Another interesting thing happened on our journey to the global village — the American family began to disintegrate.

"The new American generation is being destroyed, as if by some master plan, and parents are virtually powerless to halt the destruction. The place where children learn love and trust and belief, the sanctuary from hostile forces — the family — is changing drastically," according to Professor Urie Bronfenbrenner, head of the Department of Human Development and Family Studies, New York State College of Human Ecology, Cornell University.

"The changes are so revolutionary and threatening that many children are faced with death, suicide, crime and increased use of drugs as they struggle fiercely for survival," he said in a newspaper interview.

One youth director with whom I recently talked described his congregation as one massive collection of personal identity crises.

Homes are being ripped apart at a frightening pace. Any youth director knows that the effectiveness of the youth program is very dependent on the support of the families within the church. When those families are in disarray, that support is very often withdrawn.

If it ever was true, it certainly is no longer true that "children brought up in Sunday school are seldom brought up in court." Any judge can tell you that many of the young people who come before him for trial are children of Christian parents and many of them were once active in local churches themselves.

The bigness of everything in our society and the impersonality of contact with the whole world have created a desperate need in the lives of millions of young people for intimate relationships. The small-group concept has been proven for more than a decade to be a valid approach for establishing this kind of intimacy.

Through television and mass entertainment activities, we have become a nation of spectators. People all over America are sensing the need for deep personal involvement.

In an age when television puts a bar in many living rooms and seizes the minds of children with its violence and immorality, the church can provide wholesome entertainment for the family that is otherwise not available.

It is more difficult to communicate with young people today than ever before, but it is worth the effort. There is a quiet revolution — and sometimes not so quiet a revolution — going on in the church of Jesus Christ today. It is a positive, constructive revolution. I for one am glad to be a part of it and am hopeful that in the vernacular of youth, "you ain't seen nothin' yet." Together, we'll improve our efforts and increase our effectiveness. And as a church, we'll communicate better with today's youth.

Communicating through the Basic Needs of Youth

If we can go back to the couple on the beach at the beginning of this chapter, the expressions of love were so readily received because they spoke to the basic needs each of the two people felt. When each person spoke to the needs and desires of the other, the message was received graciously, and it produced the desired response.

There's a strong clue in that for anyone who wants to break through all the interference described earlier and communicate effectively with young people. *If you would have young people hear your messages, speak to the issues that are vital to their lives.*

In the chapter on "Understanding Young People," I talked about the basic needs of youth. Now let's see how we can use those basic needs as a means of breaking through those barriers and touching the lives of the youth in our groups.

Young People Need to Be Loved

Every major book of the last decade on child-rearing and personal development has emphasized that the greatest need a developing personality has is for a strong, positive self-image. *People need to feel that they are OK, that they have value as persons, that they are lovable.*

Perhaps more than we realize, our self-image is formed by the way we feel that other people view us. If others view us as worthwhile people, we tend to grow up feeling that we are worthwhile, that we matter. Young people tend to respond positively to people who affirm their value as human beings. And they shy away from people who put them down. Therefore, as you seek to communicate with young people, send messages that affirm their value as people.

A friend of mine told of going into a jail to visit a 15-year-old boy who had just killed a schoolmate with five bullets from a revolver.

"What do you want?" the young man asked in a surly tone.

"I'm a minister, and I'd like to help if I can," my friend replied.

"I done seen two preachers," the boy shot back with hatred. "They told me I was going to hell and that I'd sent another boy to hell."

"Look, I'm here because I love you," my friend continued. "I'd like to help in any way I can. . . . I'm not your judge. . . . Is there anything I can do?"

Almost instantly, the hostile reaction went away, and within a few minutes, the boy was sobbing on the minister's shoulder. A longtime friendship was established with a boy who needed help as much as anyone could.

"I wonder what could have been done if I had had the opportunity to say that to the boy before the shooting," the minister mused later.

All of us need to be loved, to be understood, to be accepted and counted as worthwhile human beings. And young people are no different.

The love must not only be there — it must be expressed. *I love you* may very well be the most valuable words in the English language when they are spoken with sincerity and backed up by action.

A church that makes young people feel accepted and treasured will always have a strong youth ministry.

Young People Need to Love

Sometimes it may look as if a teenager is all wrapped up in himself — that no one else in the whole world matters. Many young people find it hard to express love, to get close to anyone, or allow anyone to get close to them.

Adolescence is a time of great fear and uncertainty. Some teenagers play the game of "do unto others before they have an opportunity to do unto you." It works like this. They are afraid that if they open up and reach out to another person, their love will be rejected. So they play hard to get, or maybe just appear shy.

One girl who attended a retreat I conducted shied away from the group all weekend despite all my efforts to get her to join in. I thought she was bored. Finally, as the retreat closed and everyone was leaving, she came up to me.

"This retreat has meant more to me than anything in my whole life," she said, and turned quickly and ran away.

It was obvious that she had felt a great deal of love for me and the others in the group, but had a very difficult time expressing it.

Effective youth ministry that enables young people to open up, to reach out to others and to God, and to express feelings they have can unlock the most powerful force in the world.

Harry Emerson Fosdick once said, "To be loved is to be enobled — to love is to be inspired."

Young People Need to Be Useful — to Contribute

A well-known minister shared that the most exciting summer of his whole life was the summer he spent, along with some of the boys of his church, digging out the basement of the church to make a place for their Sunday school room.

Young people, like all of us, need to feel that they are worth something as humans. Being given responsibility, taking on a challenge or doing something important can make a young person feel that he has worth. But a very important part of involving young people is making sure that they are recognized and rewarded for what they do.

"It is often said that one-third of the world's population goes to bed hungry . . . but right here in America, millions of people go to bed every night starving for recognition," is one of my favorite quotes.

It takes so little and can mean so much to give recognition for a job well done or to offer a compliment to a teenager.

Young People Need to Grow

Isn't it exciting to see the restless, searching mind of youth at work within your group?

Young people are curious, interested, alert. They want to know everything about everything. They need to understand themselves — who they are, where they are going, what life means to them. And they need to understand the world around them.

"There are no foolish questions — only foolish answers," according to Sister Mary Corita.

Helping young people discover the realities of life is one of the most exciting challenges of youth work.

Stick to the Basics — and Communicate Effectively

"Let's get back to the basics, so we can win some games," the coach often tells his players. It's a good idea, too, for people who would communicate effectively with youth.

Often in our planning or in the dailiness of working out our plans, we concentrate on material needs, physical needs and the like. But you just watch — any youth director who shows love and enables young people to express love, who utilizes the talents and energies of youth and helps them to grow and learn, will be able to break through all the barriers and communicate effectively with them.

If you want what matters to you to be received, concentrate on what matters to the youth in your group. You'll get the desired response.

Tested and Proven Communications Techniques

Communicating with young people and with adults about young people will be your greatest challenge. If you learn to do it well, it will be a great asset to your ministry.

"She really has a way with kids," a pastor recently remarked about his church's youth director. "I don't know how she does it, but she can get them to do things nobody has ever been able to do before," he continued.

Well, let's see if we can discover those special techniques of a good communicator.

Learning to Listen

The first rule of good communication is that those who would communicate must learn to listen. Much has been said in recent years about listening as more than something you do as a courtesy to keep from interrupting the person who is talking.

Two terms that have come out of the modern search for better ways of communicating are "aggressive listening" and "active listening." They suggest that listening is something that is actively done in an effort to build a bridge over which ideas and thoughts can flow.

There are many reasons why active listening is so important. Here, I will only touch on a few:

1. ***Listening is really a great act of love.*** A minister once told of several counseling appointments with a woman who was reputed to be extremely quiet. She would come to the office with a lot of things on her mind, but was almost totally unable to express what she obviously felt very deeply. She would sometimes sit for 10 minutes without saying a word. He avoided the temptation to jump in and make conversation. Eventually she would ask a question or make a statement. At the close of the second session, she said to him, "I want to thank you for listening to me — I was beginning to wonder if anyone cared enough to hear what I had to say." And then she added, "Maybe God will listen to me after all."

Sometimes it takes all the strength you can muster to sit and listen to the silence or to the endless prattling of a youngster who is convinced that he is God's gift to the world. But it is one of the most tangible ways to say, "I love you and God loves you."

"Kids won't listen anymore" is a common cry of parents and church leaders. But many young people have said, "My parents don't hear a thing I say." These youngsters generally feel unloved.

2. **Listening helps people discover things about themselves.** Have you ever talked to a person who was always in trouble, and had him agree with everything you said, only to leave you and go do the same thing again? The truth is you may have said a lot but communicated little. There is a difference.

What you say is not nearly so important as what they learn from your time together. It is in this realm that small groups are such a powerful tool of communication. As the young people share with each other and come to feel more accepted, they will open up and reveal their false images of themselves. When they have told the group how bad they are and no one attacks them, they will often express the hope that they can be worthwhile people.

As listening becomes a way of life for you and your youth group members, they will begin to discover some deep feelings and fears that they did not know existed. When they make the discovery, rather than simply being told, they are more likely to deal with flaws and develop strengths.

3. **Active listening avoids trying to answer questions nobody is asking.** The beginning point of effective communication with a young person is that point at which he or she asks a question. Until that occurs, words are at best boring, and at worst, offensive.

Everything you say as a representative of the church is filtered through the young person's own set of notions about life and the subject at hand. Once young people feel you have really understood the problem or situation as they perceive it, they will be open to receive your input.

4. *Active listening gives people the opportunity to vent deep and painful feelings.* Have you ever seen someone driving down the road talking to himself? He may have a very angry expression on his face and really be letting it all out. Chances are that when he meets the person with whom he is angry, he will have calmed down and all will be lovely.

Most people at some time and some people at all times need to vent their pent-up feelings of anger or hurt. A few are unable to get it out by talking to themselves or kicking the dog. Many need to express those feelings to a sympathetic listener. As a friend, you and your group can do a youngster a real favor by simply hearing him out. Once the feelings are out in the open, he can deal with them more effectively. You might pick up a bonus: you might discover something that will be helpful in your efforts to deal with the hang-ups.

5. *Active listening is important because everyone needs to be heard.* Sometimes people need to say things for no other reason than that they need to say them.

The most effective tool in listening is asking questions. When in a group meeting or just "rapping" with one person, follow each statement with a question that is designed to get the other person to talk.

Questions like, "How did that make you feel" or "What was your reaction to that?" are very helpful when a youngster describes an injustice done him. You may not be able to do anything about the injustice, if in fact there was one, but you can always offer help in dealing with the way a person reacted to the injustice.

Interpreting feelings back to the person is also important as a tool of listening. This is done by using statements like, "Do you mean . . . ?" or by simply repeating in your own words what the person has said. This helps two people. It confirms for both you and the other person that you have really heard the meaning expressed.

Much more could be said on active listening, but since space is limited, let me simply say that your effectiveness as a communicator will be directly proportional to your effectiveness as a listener.

Use Simple, Precise Words

In communicating with young people, it is crucial that you use terms and symbols that are familiar to them.

A well-known evangelist was once flying into Houston, Texas, to address the student body of Southern Methodist University when his aircraft was placed in a holding pattern because of a heavy fog over the city. He became more and more nervous as the time for him to speak came and went while he was still up in the air.

"The Lord used that incident to show me something very important," he later observed. "I realized that much of my preaching was like that. While the audience was waiting on the ground to hear me, I was circling around in the fog."

Most of us spend too much time circling around in the fog when it comes to communicating with young people. Perhaps one reason that Jesus was so powerful in communicating was that he always managed to say exactly what needed to be said, when it needed to be said, with words and illustrations that the people could easily understand.

Now this does not mean that to communicate with young people you have to develop a vocabulary of words they use to impress each other with how "cool" they are. In fact, that's a dangerous game to play. First of all, using their jargon is tricky, and you are more likely to come across as stupid than you are to convince them you are cool. Secondly, that language is representative of a world they want someday to leave. They may feel threatened if you try to camp out there. Further, they may not understand all the terms they use.

What is important is that you develop a vocabulary that expresses precisely what you mean in words that most of the people in your group can understand.

Test through Feedback

One technique helpful in determining if you are really communicating what you intend is to constantly test yourself through a variety of feedback mechanisms:

- As often as you can, get the young people to say in their own words what you have said to them. If they have missed your meaning, keep trying until you have said what you intended to say.

- Exercises provide another method of testing your effectiveness as a communicator. The idea of an exercise is to determine if the audience has working knowledge of the information you have tried to communicate.

- Some youth directors like to use skits to get their young people to reenact the meat of a message or article. Translating parables into modern settings can offer you another method of determining if young people are really hearing the message of the Gospel.

Whatever methods you use, test yourself often. It is an important part of the total communications process.

Help Youth Communicate with Youth

You have probably observed that teenagers listen to each other far more readily than they will listen to an adult. One principle that might prove helpful is to never say anything you can get a teenager to say for you.

Deal Tactfully with Disruptions

It seems that in every crowd there is a wise guy who tries to block anything of a meaningful nature. He may make smart remarks, whisper to his friends, get up and walk around, or all of the above — and more.

If you are making a "one-night stand," you may have to settle for putting him in his place. However, if you have to live with that person for years to come, you need to look for more constructive approaches.

Here are some suggestions:

- View the disruption as a symptom. The person may be bored with the subject or the way it is being presented. Overt acts of disruption may express something that others feel but are too courteous to show. If what you are doing is not working, don't get upset — change your approach until you find something that works.

- Learn about the disrupter. He may be so miserable at home or school that he needs help. It is far more important to meet the needs of the disrupter than to silence the disruption. Some time spent with him at home might be a good investment.

- Learn from the disrupters. Try to discover what they do that excites the group. With a little imagination, you might be able to out-disrupt them. Remember, not only is the disrupter failing as a listener, you are failing as a communicator.

- Ask for the disrupter's help in something. Try to work with him enough so that the two of you will become a team with common goals — goals that he considers worthwhile — and mutual respect.

- If the disrupter is annoying the whole group, use the concept of positive peer pressure. Enlist the aid of the whole group in dealing with the wise guy.

Conclusion

Much more could be said about communication, but I have tried to hit the highlights. The most important thing to remember is that real love finds a way to communicate. Warmth and sincerity go a long way toward setting the pattern for effective communication. Aggressive, nonjudgmental listening can be more valuable than all the words you could utter. When it is necessary to talk, break it down into words and symbols that have meaning to the young people themselves. Handle disruptions as symptoms of deeper concerns and do what you have to to get at their roots.

GROWTH EXERCISE

Using the principles of this section, set about listening actively to at least three people to whom you normally talk a lot. Observe the impact of your listening on the people with whom you seek to communicate.

Section III

Gearing Up for Action

CHAPTER 8

Emerging Trends in Youth Ministry

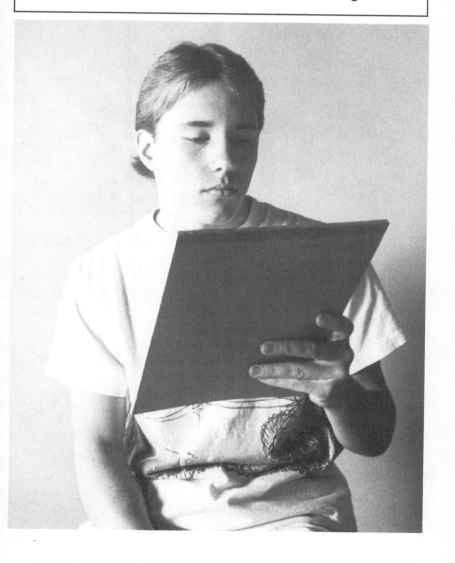

Some exciting new trends are emerging as the church moves out to recapture the interest and enthusiasm of its youth. Many churches have discovered that they must compete for attention, time and money, and they are gearing up for action.

Never before have there been so many interesting things for young people and adults to do and see. In this highly technological world, every day offers something new. Television has captured more than 30 hours per week of the typical child's life; school activities have become more challenging; entertainment has become one of the major industries in our country; and the automobile makes life easier and more pleasant than ever.

And inflation has forced many churches into tight money situations.

All this is threatening to many people. Yet there are some youth ministries that are growing by leaps and bounds and are becoming constantly more exciting. How do they do it? Those of us who supply programming materials and resources to churches have seen several major trends emerge in the last few years.

Better Programming

Many churches have worked hard at developing better programming to meet the challenge.

Never before has there been such an emphasis on training and equipping youth leaders to do their jobs. Colleges and seminaries have added courses in youth ministry and related subjects to their curricula; churches have set aside more money for scholarships and for seminars; and the electronics boom is filtering into the church to help with training volunteers.

Publishers are offering a wider range of better materials and program aids than were ever before available.

In short, it is now possible for even a small church to carry on a more effective youth ministry than could have been operated by a very large church a few years ago.

More Involvement of Youth

Planning task forces, which only a few years ago were made up almost entirely of adults, are now largely made up by young people and operating under the guidance of adults. Young people are planning their own retreats, weekly programs and camps, and even are guiding church boards as to how to better integrate the youth into the life of the church.

Much has been said to lead us to believe that today's youth are negative, apathetic and troubled. In my travels, I find that this is not so at all. Young people today are the brightest, most alert, and often the most committed to the church that they have ever been. Young people are like airplanes, however; we only hear of the ones which crash.

Churches everywhere are finding that young people can do more than anybody thought possible a few years ago. The use of youthful energy in planning and implementing the church's total program is one of the most exciting trends in the life of the church today.

More Emphasis on the Whole Person

"What can we do to top what we did last year?" was the big question for youth leaders a few years ago. Now, the challenge is to look more deeply into the needs of youth and develop ministries that most adequately meet those needs.

Youth ministers are finding that there are more studies that have been done on the needs of youth, more programs designed to develop the total person, and a greater understanding on the part of the church of youth's needs. All this has made it possible for a church to approach with more confidence and skill the cultivation of its children into truly Christian adults.

More Issue-Oriented Programming

People in general have become much more aware of the need for the church to become involved in the struggles of the world. As a result, there is more emphasis in materials and programming on such subjects as world hunger, social problems and war.

All of this may appear to be an effort to get away from the Bible. However, a close examination shows that the effort is really one to apply the Bible to life.

In churches all over the world, young people are struggling with major questions and searching for answers to dilemmas that the youth of a generation ago didn't even know existed. And the church is faced with the challenge of assuring that those answers are biblically based.

More Intimate Programming

One of the major impacts of the technological revolution has been difficulties in personal relationships. The church is rising to that challenge by providing more opportunities for people to become more intimately involved with each other.

Retreats, small groups and talent-development programs are now the bread and butter of exciting, alive youth ministries. In these groups, young people can search for solutions to the loneliness and isolation that so many of them feel.

There is a greater emphasis on getting adults in the church involved with the youth in these smaller groups. And the results have been fantastic — both for the youth and the adults.

Conclusion

Churches that want to succeed in God's ministry today must constantly stay abreast of youth's needs and the wide array of resources available to meet those needs.

I believe the church has a dynamic message for the changing world. We have always claimed that Christ is a "rock in a weary land;" we have always proclaimed him "a shelter in the time of storm;" and we have said that he is the "same yesterday, today and forever." Millions the world over are finding that to be true.

Now is the time for the church to make its voice so clear, so powerful and so exciting that it is not crowded out by all the other voices clamoring for our youth's attention.

GROWTH EXERCISE

List at least five specific changes you have seen in the youth ministries with which you have been most closely connected during the last 10 years. Write a brief analysis of factors you think have brought about those changes.

CHAPTER 9

How to Build an Exciting Youth Ministry

Young people are drawn to excitement. They enjoy being involved in activities that are fun, that touch the vital needs of their lives, that provide opportunities for them to grow and learn. Youth ministers all over America and around the world are discovering that young people will respond in large numbers and with great enthusiasm to creative programming.

But exciting youth ministries don't just happen — they are the result of strong leadership, careful planning and vigorous implementation. Step by step, the way a skilled stonemason builds a cathedral, they are put together by skillful youth leaders.

Just as a builder needs an architect's blueprint to put together a cathedral, you as a youth leader need a clear idea as to where you are going with your youth group.

Long before the first stone of a magnificent building was laid — in fact, long before the blueprint was drawn — there existed in the architect's mind an image of what the building would look like when it was completed.

I have observed that the greatest single reason youth ministries falter and remain ineffective is that they lack the clear vision of a leader who knows exactly what he is trying to accomplish. Far too many youth programs grow up by accident and resemble the village in the following fable a successful youth leader once used to illustrate to his church board how its youth program had evolved.

A Fable

Once upon a time, in a faraway land, there was a village in which people lived and worked and played and enjoyed life.

One day the village chief called all the people together and told them of a serious problem. It seemed that the well in the center of the village was drying up, and very soon there would be no water for the people to drink, cook with and use for baths and laundry. The people became worried and asked among themselves what could be done about it.

Finally, one day it happened! The well dried up completely. All the people came together to talk about what could be done.

"I have found water!" a young man from the village shouted as he ran into the gathering.

"Where?" asked the village chief.

"It is a long way off," the young man said. "It flows in a stream over in that direction."

"We must move the village," someone in the crowd said.

"No, that is impractical," someone else said.

Finally a young man stepped forward with a solution which everyone readily accepted.

"I will take clay from the bank of the stream and form it into water pots. With these we can bring enough water to meet our daily needs," he said.

All the people cheered and followed the young man to the stream, where the process of making water pots was begun.

Very carefully, the young man shaped each water pot out of clay and placed it in the sun to bake. Soon there were enough water pots for each family in the village, and a new tradition was begun.

Every morning and every evening, the young people of the village went to the stream and filled the water pots and brought them back to their homes.

After many years, the young man who had fashioned the water pots, who now was a very old man, died and was buried in the village graveyard.

"Let us build a monument to the man whose idea saved our village," said the village chief.

So all the people came together and erected a huge water pot in the center of the village. The people all fell down and paid homage to the monument and expressed their gratitude for having plenty of water to meet their needs.

Many centuries later, a young man who called himself a Peace Corps worker came to the village. He said that he had come to help the people have a better way of life. He offered to teach them better ways to grow crops, to build sanitation systems, and to teach their children to read and write.

"There is no time for all of that," said the village chief. "The children must spend hours each day going to and from the stream to fetch water."

"Why don't you dig a canal and channel the water from the stream into the village?" the young outsider asked. "It is all downhill and the water would flow freely," he said.

"No!" shouted the people with one accord. "We cannot do that!"

"My great-great-grandfather fashioned the water pots with his own hands," a young man said.

"My father carried this water pot before me and his father before him and his father before him. We will never abandon our water pots."

The young outsider persisted, and the villagers grew more angry. Finally they jerked him up and nailed him to a tree, where he was rescued by some other Peace Corps workers.

As the Peace Corps workers started running away from the village, they heard all the people gathered around the water pot in the center of the village, singing songs and dancing in honor of their great leader who had built the water pots.

The End.

We need only to substitute the words *youth program* in place of *water pot* to see how some churches have developed their youth ministries. Their primary reason for everything they do is, "That's the way we've always done it!" Ask them why the youth of their church are not more excited by the programs and activities, and they'll likely say, "Young people today are just too self-centered. . . . All they want is a good time!"

I'll let you in a secret: *People of all ages do not back "good causes;" they respond to effective leadership toward goals they believe are worthwhile!*

Targeted Programming

Join me in a little word association game that could radically change your outlook on programming for youth.

When I say the word *target*, what's the first image that comes into your mind? *"Bullseye!"* That's right — you've got it! Effective youth leaders have learned that everything they do must be aimed at accomplishing specific goals.

Why Set Goals?

1. *The best reason to set goals is that it is exactly what Jesus did, and he's our great example.* The plan of salvation was formulated in the mind of God long before Jesus was ever born in a manger. Someone has noted that "the cross of Jesus was not just the result of evil action by wicked men; it was the fulfillment of the plan of God, laid before the foundation of the earth."

   I suggest that you spend some time rereading the four Gospels with this in mind. You will be amazed at how many times Jesus indicated that he did nothing by accident or whim, but that everything he did was by a plan carefully calculated to accomplish specific goals. If Jesus set goals and then took action to reach those goals, it must be a very good idea.

2. *A second reason to set specific goals in youth programming is that doing so enables you to concentrate all your efforts in a specific direction.* Have you ever noticed the difference between a swamp and a river? A swamp has shallow water that seems to try to go everywhere at once — it rambles all over the place. Its murky water provides bogs, quicksand and a breeding ground for snakes, alligators and all kinds of vermin.

   But a river runs deep; it follows a narrow and prescribed course; and it moves in a specific direction. It can be dammed up to generate electricity; its waters remain fresh; and along its banks crops grow, giant industries spring up, and large cities are built.

   Youth ministries that wander all over the place like swamps breed confusion, conflict and discontent. But youth ministries that operate on specific and worthwhile goals like rivers produce life, vitality and action.

3. *Another good reason for setting goals in youth ministry is that goals help you concentrate all your energies and resources for maximum power.* When I was a little boy, my brother gave me a magnifying glass with a handle on it. I soon

learned that I could do all kinds of tricks with it. My favorite trick was to burn holes in things by using the glass to concentrate all the sun's rays into a powerful beam. It was always thrilling to see the small spot where the sun's rays were focused begin to smoke, and then burst into flames.

But I discovered much more than how to burn holes in things from that little object lesson. I discovered that concentrated power can be used to mobilize all my energies, talents and resources to maximum advantage.

Even the smallest churches have many resources that can be used productively in ministering to its youth if a youth leader can channel all those resources toward a specific set of goals. Conversely, even the largest churches do not have enough resources to do a good job with their youth programs unless those resources are directed at specific targets.

4. ***Setting goals helps you make the most of the time available to you.*** Each of us has only 1,440 minutes each day, and in most youth ministries, youth leaders fritter away much of that time trying to accomplish too many things.

"The hurrier I go the behinder I get," reads the sign in the office of one harried youth director I know. She stays on the run all the time, and still feels that there is "never enough time."

If you feel that you don't have enough time to do all the things you believe you should, I have good news and I have bad news.

First the bad news: There's not going to be any more time! Now for the good news: You don't need any more time — if you will take maximum advantage of your minutes by concentrating on specific goals.

Harried, ineffective youth leaders concentrate on action, but effective youth leaders concentrate on goals. That's why the effective youth leaders always seem to have enough time to get everything done — and still have time left over to spend with their families, on hobbies and on self-development.

5. ***Setting goals helps other people know how to help you complete your tasks.*** No one is talented enough and energetic enough to carry on an effective youth program alone. We all need all the help we can get. And interestingly, there are always plenty of people willing to help the youth, providing they can figure out what you are trying to accomplish. When you understand exactly what you are trying to do, it is easier to explain it to others, and to lead them as to how they can help you.

6. ***Setting goals enables you to monitor your progress.*** Someone once said, "If you don't know where you're going, you won't know when you get there!" That person was absolutely on target.

   The person who sets up specific targets and measures progress by how many of those targets are hit, can much more easily determine what works and what doesn't work.

   In youth ministry, the stakes are far too high for us to aimlessly shoot the "Gospel gun," never really knowing what we are accomplishing. As we rifle in on specific targets, we can produce better results, and we can use those results to convince church leaders that their resources are being used well.

7. ***Goals can help us build enthusiasm in ourselves and in young people.*** It might be difficult for us to get excited about "just another youth program or retreat" that happens to be scheduled, but if we have goals we want to accomplish with that retreat or program, we can see how it fits into the total picture. As we reach that goal, it will give us momentum to move toward the next goal with greater enthusiasm.

   Likewise, young people like to accomplish things. When they are given specific goals, and reach those goals, they can more easily be excited to take on new challenges.

   Some youth leaders and youth group members feel let down after a great victory. That is usually because the victory is isolated and has little meaning in the overall goals at which the leader is aiming. When you and the youth see every activity as a part of an exciting plan that is aimed at specific targets, it is easier to keep those excitement levels high.

How Do You Set Goals?

We have focused on why it is so important to set goals, but many people don't know how to set productive and worthwhile goals. Here are some pointers I have found helpful:

1. ***Set goals that are in keeping with the needs and interests of your group.*** A goal is important only to the extent that it is backed up by the interest of those who must fulfill it.

   "Help people discover what they want and they will move heaven and earth to get it," said one of the best salesmen who ever lived. Nowhere is that more true than with young people.

   I have seen young people accomplish amazing feats when they were working toward a goal that really mattered to them. Interestingly, in those groups where young people are excited about reaching a specific goal, discipline problems go out the window.

   Let me give you the Nido Qubein principle of successful discipline: *Desire is the key to all discipline — especially self-discipline.* When you, your helpers and the young people in your group are all committed to the goals that you have set together, discipline problems will be minimal.

   The effective youth leader understands the basic needs of all young people and the specific needs and desires of the youth within his or her own group, and keeps in touch with his own personal needs and interests. Thus, goals can be set that will muster the full support of all concerned.

   If you want to set productive goals, set goals that will enable your church and its young people to accomplish what is important to them.

2. ***Set realistic goals.*** Goals that are set too low fail to sufficiently challenge you and the youth in your group. On the other hand, goals that are set too high become discouraging.

   Of course, no one can tell you what goals are realistic for you and your group, but here is a good rule of thumb: *Set goals that are somewhat, but not too much, higher than what the group accomplished last year.*

For example, don't try to double your attendance in one year, unless there are new factors present that make doing so a realistic goal. It is usually better to set a goal of increasing attendance 15 percent each year. If you can gain 15 percent each year for the next five years, you can double the size of your youth group.

Always keep goals low enough to be achievable, but high enough to be challenging.

3. *Set quantifiable goals.* One reason people tend to lose sight of their goals is that those goals are so general that they lose their meaning.

Let me illustrate. It is usually much more productive to say, "I'm going to read 24 books during the coming year," than it is to say, "I'm going to read everything I have time to read." By setting a specific goal, you will be able to set aside the time to reach that goal.

Get very specific with your goals — both on a personal level and with the people in your youth group. Make sure everybody knows exactly what you want to do in the set time frame.

4. *Write down your goals and review them periodically.* If a goal is worth setting, it is worth putting in writing. In fact, that is the only way you will be able to keep your goals in focus.

For many years now, I have written down a complete set of personal goals at the beginning of each new year, and made it a regular part of my routine to set aside time to review how much progress I am making toward those goals. To do otherwise is to waste time on things demanded of me by circumstances and other people.

5. *Set a specific target date for completion of your goals.* I have found that if I plan to do something in a general way, when I get around to it, then it never gets done. If I write down exactly what I plan to accomplish and the date by which I plan to accomplish it, I usually get it done on time.

This also helps in motivating other people. By giving people deadlines by which I want them to have completed specific tasks, I can motivate them to meet those deadlines. They feel a sense of accomplishment, and the goal is met.

6. ***Break your goals down into specific, manageable tasks.*** Few of us can qualify to wear a big *S* on our jerseys. We are human beings with definite limitations. The secret to getting things done personally and motivating others to get things done is to break down the goals into specific tasks that can be done readily.

For example, if we can go back to the goal of reading 24 books during the next year, if you break that down so that you are reading two books each month, you are a lot more likely to achieve it. You will be even further ahead if you can select the 24 books in advance and set up a reading schedule. Of course, you will want to allow for new books coming out, and plan to make substitutions as desired.

7. ***Use your goals as a basis for evaluating your progress.*** At the end of the time you have set, check to see that you have met all your goals. Celebrate and commend those who have helped you reach the goals you have met. Determine why any goal has not been met and set up a plan for reaching that goal.

Remember, winners make their goals, losers make excuses; winners concentrate on goals, losers concentrate on activities.

8. ***Use your goals as a platform for setting new goals.*** Once you have reached your goals, always use those goals as a basis for setting new goals.

One of the most beautiful realities of God's living creation is that we can always be reaching out to take on new challenges. I have found that the best way to stay alert and to keep my zest for living is to pause briefly to thank God for his help in reaching my goals and then ask for his help in reaching out for new goals.

What Is an Effective Youth Program?

Webster defines *effective* as *producing a definite and desired result.* In other words, an effective youth ministry is one that gets the results you want to achieve.

It matters little whether your youth ministry produces a lot of action, draws a lot of people, or spends a lot of money — unless that is how you define success in youth programming.

In my estimation, the measure of a youth program's effectiveness is in the impact it has on the lives of the people it serves, the church which conducts it, and the community in which it operates. If it produces the desired results in each of those arenas, it is a success; if it does not produce the desired results in any of those arenas, it is a failure.

Jesus made it quite clear that he expects those of us who labor in his vineyard to "bring forth fruit." He expects us to get results. And he continually gives us the resources with which to get those results.

Effectiveness: A Profile

To be very concrete, let's zero in on some specifics of the kind of results a youth ministry should produce. To do that, we will look at a profile of an effective youth ministry, keeping in mind our definition of such a ministry from the chapter on "Youth Ministry in Perspective."

Mobilize the Full Resources of the Church for Maximum Benefit

Notice that I did not say *motivate,* but rather, *mobilize* the full resources of the church. Motivation is only one part of the overall task of mobilizing all the resources available to do an effective job of reaching youth with the Gospel.

There are at least four tasks for the youth leader in mobilizing the resources of the church:

- The leader must assess the resources to determine what is available to meet the needs of the planned youth program.

- The youth leader must plan for an effective use of the resources made available.

- The leader must motivate the leaders and members of the church to commit as many resources as possible to the youth ministry.

- The youth leader must manage the resources committed by organizing and directing their use.

It is quite likely that your church will never commit as many resources to youth ministry as you would like. However, two of the most common failures of youth directors are: first, they fail to assess, plan and motivate the available resources; second, they fail to adequately manage the resources that are committed.

There are two kinds of resources available to the youth leader — physical resources and people resources.

Physical resources consist of buildings, equipment, money and printed materials. These are the tools the youth minister must use in carrying out the youth program.

Mobilizing these resources calls for a management expertise that many youth leaders simply don't have. I would suggest that you make an in-depth study of the management of resources — at the local library or a nearby college or in the many books available on the subject. Unfortunately, far too many youth directors are satisfied to let the available physical resources manage the youth program, rather than managing the resources to fit the needs of the youth ministry.

Often when a youth director complains to me that he lacks the physical resources to adequately carry out the church's program, I find that the real problem is that the church has not been fully informed as to the needs and plans for use of the resources requested. When you have said, "We don't have enough money," or "Our building is just not big enough," all you have done is to state the problem. As a youth leader it is your task to develop strategies for solving those problems.

People resources include any person or groups of people within your church who might contribute in any way to the success of your youth ministry.

Since we will look much more closely at managing people resources in a later section, let me say only that of all the challenges facing the youth minister, success or failure in this area is usually the greatest determining factor in the success or failure of a youth ministry.

Bring Young People into a Vital Relationship with Christ

Many of today's youth programs are little more than extracurricular activities for the youth. The emphasis is almost entirely on having fun, keeping the young people busy doing things, and providing enough entertainment to draw big crowds.

As part of the church of Jesus Christ, the local youth program is a unique entity in the lives of young people. It, more than any other group, has the opportunity — and the responsibility — to introduce young people to the reality of the Christ which the Christian church preaches.

Now, there is a lot more to that task than simply preaching — even with a youth emphasis. What we are talking about is bringing young people into a vital relationship with the living Christ.

Doing so involves presenting the Gospel in a creative and challenging way that touches the lives of young people. It involves providing opportunities for young people to respond to Christ on a very personal level. And it involves helping them assimilate that Gospel into the daily experience of their lives.

There are at least two dimensions to every effective youth ministry. First, there is the ministry to the youth of the church — the children of the church members and other young people who have become involved in the church. Second, there is the outreach to other young people in the community in which the church serves.

Those youth programs that have been most successful have been the ones that take seriously the young people of the church and, with their help, reach out to try to touch as many young lives in the community as possible.

The content of a lively, effective youth ministry must be the Gospel of Jesus Christ as it relates to the daily lives of the youth it serves. The result of an effective youth ministry is that its participants come into the fullness of God's life, and develop into a redemptive community in which people find support and help as they seek to grow into a deeper relationship with Christ.

The measure of success is not to be found in the numbers of teens who show up for activities but in the quality of spiritual growth experienced by those who participate.

It is interesting to note, however, that in those groups where spiritual and emotional maturity are evident, numbers do tend to increase substantially. Vast numbers of people in our world are looking for the vitality and joy of a deep personal relationship with Christ. They will go where life is.

Provide Opportunities for Growth

One of the most exciting aspects of serving as a youth leader is assisting young people in the process of growing — both in their spiritual lives and toward their full potential as human beings.

But that growth doesn't take place by accident; it comes as a result of carefully planned and vigorously implemented programming. A good, growth-oriented youth ministry contributes to growth in at least the five ways listed below:

- *It initiates growth.* As Christ called his disciples to grow toward greater maturity in him, so we are to constantly issue the call for young people to grow to full maturity in Christ.

- *It stimulates growth.* The effective youth leader is one who knows how to create a desire in young people to reach out and claim their full heritage as children of God.

- *It supports while they are growing.* Growth is often a painful and frustrating process for the young. The effective youth leader, like the tender shepherd, undergirds those who are struggling and assures them that the growth is worth the effort.

- *It helps young people clarify issues of life.* There is so much ambiguity in moral questions today that many young people grow up confused as to how to deal with the major issues they face every day. An effective youth ministry instills those mechanisms for clarifying issues in an ever-changing world.

- *It helps young people develop values and builds value clarification systems.* Many adults today are struggling through spiritual identity crises because they never learned how to sort out the many voices that clamor for their attention. An effective youth ministry instills in young people a set of values that can guide them through life, and a system for applying the Bible to daily experiences.

Perhaps the apostle Paul best defined the goal of all Christian growth in Ephesians 4:13:

So shall we at last attain to the unity inherent in our faith and our knowledge of the Son of God — to mature manhood, measured by nothing less than the full stature of Christ. (New English Bible)

Any youth ministry that leads its youth to that kind of development can be called very effective.

Provide a Foundation for Career
Choices and Healthy Attitudes

The Christian church has always maintained that God is interested in both the attitudes with which people face life and the directions they pursue in their careers.

One of the biggest challenges that a typical young person faces today is the choice as to how he will invest the talents God has given him. Making the choice is a confusing task because there are so many opportunities from which to pick.

An effective youth ministry does not seek to tell young people what they should do with their lives. Instead, it seeks to help them sort through the issues involved, analyze their feelings and needs, and develop mechanisms for making satisfying choices.

Further, an effective youth ministry stimulates young people to reach as high as they can reach to fulfill their destiny as human beings.

Nothing matters more to a young person coming to adulthood than the attitudes that he takes into life — regardless of what career he chooses.

An effective youth ministry seeks to graduate its members with at least the following ingredients for a successful life:

- *A strong, positive self-image:* It instills a feeling of worth and value, a feeling that the person matters and has a place in the universe.

- *A strong sense of self-confidence:* It develops the attitude that a person has capabilities, strengths and talents, and can make a valuable contribution to the world.

- *A strong feeling of self-reliance:* It cultivates a person's willingness to stand on his own two feet and become a contributing member of society and the church.

- *A positive mental attitude:* Soon enough, the negative forces of life will exert pressure. A good youth ministry helps people cultivate the habit of seeing life optimistically.

- *Self-discipline:* The mature young person knows that there will come a time when there is no one to tell him what to do. Those who have been adequately ministered to will discipline themselves.

- *An ability to communicate effectively:* Through repeated opportunities to communicate with others and through instruction, the effective youth ministry teaches young people how to communicate adequately.

- *An ability to draw on the infinite resources of God:* More than any other group, a youth ministry has the opportunity to help young people grow up knowing how to pray, and to use the resources God gives so freely.

- *An ability to relate to others:* While a mature young person feels he has a place in the universe, he knows that place is not at the center of that universe. A good youth ministry teaches its members how much we all need others, and how to receive through giving to others.

- *A strong sense of connection with all mankind:* An effective youth ministry cultivates an awareness of each person's kinship with all other members of God's creation.

Strengthen Relationships in the Lives of Young People

Ours is the most connected world in history. We have instant and mass communication systems that could enable us to establish strong relationships with peoples of all nations and all walks of life. Unfortunately, we have not yet learned how to use these mechanisms effectively in building good relationships. Our world is, paradoxically, the most disconnected world in history.

No task of a youth ministry is more important than that of helping young people to build strong and rewarding relationships with their families, their church and the world in which they live.

In far too many youth programs, the young people are isolated from all but the very restrictive age group into which they fall. The idea of separating people by age groups sounds good, but in practice, it has the effect of restricting the contact of young people to others their own age, and robs them of the opportunity to learn how to relate satisfactorily to older or younger people.

To correct this problem, many youth ministries are shifting their emphasis to a totally integrated family/church/world programming approach. While they still maintain some programs that are segregated by age levels, much of their programming is done in three areas: family ministries, church/youth ministries and world ministries.

Whether you go with the "whole-life development" approach or a more separated youth program, it is a good idea to create as many opportunities as possible for young people to be involved with adults. Every effort must be made to strengthen their relationships in each of the following areas:

- *Family relationships:* An effective youth ministry helps young people find ways to resolve conflicts with their parents and other siblings, to relate positively to family members, and to prepare for life in a family of their own.

- *Church relationships:* An important part of growing up is finding a rewarding and useful place within a local worship community. It is crucial that the youth ministry help young people find a place to plug into the worship and service activities of the church.

- *Relationships with the world:* The Christian church holds definite views of the world at all levels — intimate friendships, the workplace, the city, the nation and the whole world. Imparting this Christian view and developing mechanisms for dealing with the issues raised by the various levels of contact are vital functions of an effective youth ministry.

Contribute to Church Worship Life and Local and International Service

Increasingly, churches are recognizing the valuable contribution that young people can make to the ongoing ministries of the church at all levels.

Teenagers have a great deal to offer to the church community in all aspects of its ministry:

- They have a way of focusing questions, though sometimes rather painfully, that forces the church to take a serious look at what it is doing in the community and why. The fresh questioning of all the ministries of the church can be very healthy.

- Young people can bring an invigorating liveliness to adult activities such as worship, service and small groups. Adults need to have fun as much as young people, and where young people show up, fun has a tendency to happen.

- Teenagers seem to have boundless energy which can be channeled into the fulfillment of the church's ministries and outreaches.

- The current crop of teenagers is probably the most talented and capable crop ever to hit the scene. In worship activities, their talents can provide a freshness and spiritual vitality that can be very refreshing to a staid old congregation. In the realm of family entertainment, teenagers can come up with more ideas than the church can ever implement.

- Often churches are amazed to discover the capabilities that teenagers have for solving some of the basic problems the adults have struggled with for years. Sometimes, nothing more than a fresh point of view can offer much-needed solutions.

Any church that opens itself to the possibility of extensive contact between teenagers and adults is in for a frightening but exciting experience. Something happens when teenagers and adults are put together in the context of the redemptive community that cannot happen any other way.

Conclusion

We have talked about the need for setting goals and how to set them; we have pointed out the need for targeting your programming efforts in specific directions for definite purposes; and we have discussed some worthwhile goals and targets.

As you think about the youth group with which you are most familiar, it might be helpful to evaluate that group against the definition and profile we gave of an effective youth ministry.

Further, as you look toward your own plans for leading a group of young people, you might want to set specific goals to enable you to lead your group to become effective — as outlined in the profile. There might be some elements you consider desirable that you would want to add to the profile.

We now turn our attention to the all-important task of organizing and directing an effective youth program.

GROWTH EXERCISE

There are two parts to this exercise:

1. *If you have not set goals for your personal life and for your work with youth, review the section on setting goals and set some very definite goals for the next year. If you have set goals, go back and evaluate those goals against the criteria listed in the section titled "How Do You Set Goals?"*

2. *As you review the profile of an effective youth ministry, make a list of at least three examples of how the church where you grew up followed (or did not follow) each of the six points listed in the profile. Develop a plan to show how each could work in the church with which you are now involved.*

CHAPTER 10

How to Organize for Effective Youth Ministry

The day of the Lone Ranger in youth ministry is gone forever —
if it ever existed. Does that mean that there is no place in the church
for a strong youth leader? No, indeed! It simply means that the
emphasis must be placed on *leading* others, rather than doing everything yourself.

No one is talented enough, able to be in enough places, or wise
enough to conduct an effective youth ministry alone. We all need all
the help we can get.

You can only use the resources available to you when you
organize. Simply stated, *if you would be effective as a youth leader,
get yourself and your youth program organized!*

In this chapter we will focus on two important questions: Why
should you organize? How should you organize?

Why Should You Organize?

The word *organize* scares some youth workers half to death.
It carries for them the image of strait-jacket structures, of endless
meetings, of stifled creativity, and — perhaps most of all — of
limiting God.

The precise opposite is true. Good organization eliminates
those problems, and many more.

"I don't have time for organization," some youth directors
have said. "I'm too busy dealing with emergencies."

Urgent vs. Important

One reason that so many youth directors are frustrated, tense
and ineffective is that they spend all their time dealing with those
things that are *urgent*. They wait until things develop into full-
scale emergencies before addressing them.

As a result, they spend all their time playing the firefighter —
running around putting out fires that should not have been started

to begin with. Ask them a year later what they were doing on a given date, and they can't tell you. They may be liked, but are seldom respected as leaders.

Effective youth leaders concentrate on what is *important*. They decide how they will spend their time, rather than allowing the circumstances that arise to dictate how they will spend their time.

Another way of saying it is: *Winners concentrate on what's important; losers concentrate only on what's urgent.*

Twelve Good Reasons to Organize

God operates through order. Paul points directly at the crux of the matter in 1 Corinthians 14:40. "Let all be done decently and in order," he says.

Jesus was a master organizer. When he was given the task of spreading the Gospel throughout the whole world, he did not set about to do it alone. He chose 12 people. Then he spent more than three years training, equipping and instructing them as to what they should do after he was crucified.

In the daily process of life, he used some of the most effective methods of leadership through organization:

- He delegated authority by assigning specific responsibilities. (He sent out the missionary teams, appointed a treasurer, assigned the task of preparing the Passover feast.)

- He directed activities. (Before he turned the water into wine he gave specific instructions to fill the water pots, and before he fed the multitude he instructed the disciples to have the people sit down "in companies.")

- Everything he did was done in a prearranged plan which was "laid before the foundation of the world."

If you question the notion that God works through order, look through an electron microscope sometime at the submolecular structure of even the simplest of matter, or study the massive galaxies of our solar system. You will discover in both the smallest particles of life and the most expansive reaches of space that everything God does is done "decently and in order."

Youth ministries that remain disorganized because they "don't want to restrict God's spontaneity" fail to take advantage of his creativity through structure.

Effective youth ministries find that God works best through organization, and see their planning as a strong expression of faith that God will do his part.

Organization gives people opportunities to help. "I didn't know what to do," is the most common reason people give for failing to get involved in worthwhile youth ministries. Why did they not know what to do? Usually it was because a disorganized youth director failed to give them specific tasks and instructions.

Effective youth leaders learn that not only do they need a lot of help from many people, there are many people who want to help. By organizing, they can break down tasks into bite-sized activities that those people can do.

There is a bonus to this one — people who find places to help, and give of themselves freely, benefit greatly from the experience. Reaching out to give a helping hand to a growing youngster is one of the most rewarding experiences for adults.

In the typical church, some of the most valuable resources for shaping young lives are wasted because a disorganized youth director fails to put those people resources into structures in which they can contribute something worthwhile.

Effective youth leaders organize so that they can utilize every person who is willing to contribute in any way to the success of the youth program.

Organization saves time for all involved. Wasted time, unnecessary motion, duplication of efforts, and procrastination can sap the life out of the best of youth programs.

For example, you've been talking up a big retreat and the young people are all excited. At the appointed time they show up ready to go, and the bus runs out of gas on the way to the church — because someone failed to plan for getting it serviced. You have to reschedule your arrival activities, the kids get bored and irritable, and all your excitement goes down the drain.

With careful planning and responsible execution, most of the emergencies that arise can be eliminated — or at least minimized. Time is your most valuable asset.

Organization saves resources. When Jesus fed the 5,000 people, the last thing he had the disciples do was to pick up the 12 baskets of leftovers. The Bible doesn't tell us what he did with them, but we can easily assume that he didn't waste them.

Good stewardship calls for the maximum utilization of all the physical and material resources which are assigned to a youth ministry.

Only through good organization can a youth leader make maximum usage of the resources that are assigned — or otherwise available. For example, by ordering enough literature far enough in advance, a youth director can avoid the cost of running in to make extra copies — even if the copier comes under someone else's budget.

Most youth ministries that complain of limited resources could make much better use of the resources they are given. But they can only do that when they are organized.

Organization gives you control. "I guess we're doing pretty well — under the circumstances," is a typical response of youth directors who are disorganized.

The good news of the Gospel is that, as Christians, we are not controlled by circumstances. We are given the power and the resources to control circumstances.

"You've done your homework," is one of the greatest compliments church leaders can pay to a youth director. By organizing, that youth leader goes into every meeting with clear ideas of what should be accomplished and how to get it done. Thus, he finds the church leaders much more willing to cooperate than does the person who simply responds to what takes place in the meetings.

By organizing, we can initiate the actions we want to take place, rather than reacting to what has happened. Organized youth leaders make things happen; disorganized youth leaders wait for things to happen.

Organization reduces conflict. In disorganized programs the emphasis is on fixing blame, but in organized programs the emphasis is on fixing problems and taking advantage of opportunities.

Carefully planned and well-organized activities tend to be more effective and to run much more smoothly than do disorganized activities. Thus, people are given the opportunity to share in the victory of success, rather than being forced to try to find someone to blame for failure.

Another benefit of organizing is that people tend to be happier, work more dependably, and be more cooperative when they know exactly what is expected of them and are adequately prepared to do it.

Even the young people are happier and easier to control when things go smoothly because they are carefully planned and organized. Many of the discipline problems that characterize disorganized groups could be eliminated through organization.

Organization allows for spontaneity. The youth director who has carefully planned and organized each activity is free to interact with the young people and adult volunteers. There is not the worry of how to correct a problem that wasn't allowed for in the planning, nor the confusion of not having enough volunteers, nor the frustration of not having enough resources.

It is this freedom to interact with people that provides for creativity and spontaneity in youth programming. Young people enjoy being around adults who are relaxed, who are in control, and who know what is going to happen next.

The life and vitality of a youth group can be greatly curtailed by buildings that are too cold, food that is bad or late arriving, equipment that doesn't work, etc. Good organizing techniques can greatly lower the frequency with which these life-crushers occur.

When simple tasks, unanticipated events and interruptions are held to a minimum through good planning, activities are free to come alive.

Organization allows you to adjust for emergencies. A carefully thought-out plan allows for the unexpected and determines in advance what steps will be taken if the unexpected occurs.

For example, I don't plan to have a flat tire on my way to an important speaking engagement, but I do always carry a spare tire and jack so that I can deal with that flat if it does occur. Building "spare tire" plans for youth activities can enable you to salvage many of those emergencies that can turn a youth activity into a disaster.

When Plan A fails for some good reason, you simply pull out Plan B and go right on with the activity. If a scheduled resource person doesn't show up, you simply pull out the alternate activity, and keep things moving.

Effective youth leaders know it is always easier to adjust to a well-conceived plan than it is to pull a rabbit out of a hat when the unexpected occurs.

Organization helps you avoid stress and tension. One of the greatest causes for burnout by youth workers and volunteers is undue stress and the tension it creates. Much of that stress and tension could be eliminated by careful planning and organization.

"Under pressure" is the way many youth directors describe their jobs. They work themselves into a frenzy, put in long days and endless weeks, stay worried about what is not getting done, and complain a lot.

Effective youth leaders know that they can reduce the stress of their jobs, make everyone around them much happier, and have time to relax by scheduling themselves and all activities realistically — and living by the schedules they set.

Many volunteers who give a year or two to the youth program, then burn out and quit, could be salvaged for many years of pleasant and rewarding service if youth leaders reduced stress and tension through good organization.

Organization sets a pattern for growth. Growing and thriving youth groups usually got that way because someone came up with a specific plan for building attendance and participation in youth activities. Those that are stymied in their growth usually got that way because no one had time to plan for growth.

An old story illustrates how it often comes about. A man was sent by his company to supervise the draining of a swamp in Louisiana. After several weeks with no report, the company sent him a telegram reading, "ADVISE PROGRESS ON DRAINING SWAMP." Soon came the following response in a wire: "NO TIME TO DRAIN SWAMP. UP TO WAIST IN ALLIGATORS."

Exciting youth activities attract young people. But that excitement must be built into the activities through careful planning. Also, careful planning and organization allows the youth leader time to concentrate on how to build attendance and set a pattern for growth.

Organization provides a basis for evaluation. If you know what you want to take place, you have some basis for evaluating whether or not it takes place. This gives you valuable information for future planning.

By evaluating everything you do, you can eliminate what is not effective, and concentrate on those things that produce the desired effect. But in order to know what is effective, you need to know what you are trying to accomplish and what methods you are using to accomplish it. This information only comes when you build in evaluation mechanisms during your planning stage.

Organization sets a good example. Young people learn from watching adults in action. When the youth in your group see that you take the program seriously enough to spend time and energy planning and organizing, they are more likely to take that program seriously.

Likewise, volunteers will key their interest and commitment to the interest and commitment they see you bring to organization and planning.

If you are always showing up late, putting things off, and sloppily putting activities together, don't be surprised if that's the kind of response you get from the youth and volunteers around you.

But when young people and adult volunteers see you demonstrate the advantages of careful planning and organization, they are a lot more likely to pitch in to help, to plan and organize what they do, and to invite their friends to share activities with them.

Why Organize?

I've given you 12 good reasons for organizing. The list could be greatly expanded, but I think you get the point.

"I'm just not an organized person," one youth director said to me during a seminar.

"That's a cop-out," I responded. I then explained that organization is not a personality trait, it is a cultivated habit — you have to work at it.

In fact, disorganization, procrastination and wasting time are also habits that we develop through practice. They are like weeds in a garden — they will grow up automatically, and we can only get rid of them through constantly and consciously practicing good organizational habits.

It is not at all unrealistic to expect that you can increase your effectiveness in shaping lives by 50 percent — or even double it — by improving your planning and organizing practices.

How Should You Organize?

To organize is "to arrange or form into a complete and functioning whole; to arrange by systematic planning and united effort." In his typical teenage style, one youngster defined it as "taking charge and making things happen." Still another definition is "planning your work and working your plan." Whichever definition you choose, organizing involves three basic parts: planning, implementing your plans and monitoring them. We will take them one at a time and discuss and how to do each effectively.

Planning: Your Roadmap

Just as you would not start out on a journey across the United States without a map, it is a foolish waste of your abilities, resources and God-given opportunities to tear off in youth ministry without carefully planning what you will do.

To make it easy to understand, let's break down the planning process into five steps and take them one at a time.

Assess Needs and Resources: If you would be successful at youth leadership, the first step is to determine the needs and interests of the young people you would lead, and the resources you have for meeting those needs.

"There's too much aimless shooting of the Gospel gun," someone once observed.

It reminds me of the little boy who came running home and told his mother, "Johnny fell into the pool, but I couldn't give him mouth-to-mouth resuscitation like you told me!"

"Why not?" asked the concerned mother.

"He kept jumping up and running off!" came the bewildered reply.

Young people will only support and benefit from youth programs that are designed to meet their needs and appeal to their interests. Remember that good advice from the successful salesman: "Help people discover what they want, and they will move heaven and earth to get it."

How do you design an effective youth program? First you study the needs and interests of the youth in your group. Here are some tips to help you do that:

1. *Study the basic needs of youth* from Chapter 5 of this book and read everything you can about the needs and interests of all young people.

2. *Explore the needs of your youth* by talking to church leaders, your pastor and Sunday school teachers.

3. *Ask parents what needs and interests their children have* that can be met by the youth ministry.

4. *Explore needs and interests* with the young people themselves.

5. *Listen, observe everything and make notes constantly.*

As you collect all the information from the sources listed, watch for recurring patterns, needs that keep coming up, and ideas that seem to creatively touch the lives of young people. Keep an open mind.

Next, you need to study what resources are available to meet the needs you have uncovered. Make an accurate list of all the available resources: money, buildings, equipment, people, etc.

Don't overstate your poverty. Look especially at the talents of the people who are available to help. Some of those people might have specialized talents or skills, or possessions that can add a dimension to your youth activities. Look for an artist, or a photographer, a farmer, a pilot, a drama teacher or a coach — anyone with special skills you could use effectively.

Make notes constantly about the people you meet who have something interesting they could offer your youth group. For example, a youth leader in my hometown of High Point, North Carolina, put together a contest for an outreach ministry. The grand prize was a trip for a family of four to Disneyworld — 700 miles away. The net cost to the agency was zero, because everything was done for free; including a round-trip flight in a private plane that was donated by a local industry. Even the tickets were furnished by a local merchant.

Be realistic — don't count on resources until you have them committed. But don't be afraid to go after them. The worst most people will say when given an opportunity to help is *no,* and many times they will say *yes.*

Once you have made a thorough inventory of the needs and interests of your youth and the resources for meeting those needs and appealing to those interests, you are ready for the next step in planning.

Set Goals and Priorities: You might want to review the section of the last chapter on how to set goals and use that as a guide for developing your youth programs.

Remember, you cannot do everything. Thus it is important that you decide in advance which ideas and needs get priority. Otherwise, you will water down your efforts so much that nothing worthwhile will be accomplished.

Let me suggest that you set two types of goals:

Long-range goals: These are the guiding goals that give direction to your youth program over a period of five to 10 years. They can help move you along in a clear and chosen direction.

Short-range goals: These are based on your long-range goals, and will help you steer a course for a year or six months.

By setting goals, you can select the targets at which you will aim during the specified time. This will enable you to decide what resources you will allocate to reaching the targets. Remember: *be very specific*.

Once you have decided what you are going to concentrate on, you are ready to select the priority you want to give to each of the goals. Decide which is your number-one priority of the goals you have selected, and rank each of the others in descending order.

The higher the priority rating, the greater the resources it should get. As you use the priority ratings you will be able to determine how much time, energy, talent and material resources you should set aside for each of the goals. By deciding in advance, you won't waste a lot of time on lower priorities and have to rush through the higher goals.

When you have decided what you want to accomplish, and which of the goals should get top priority, you are ready for the next step.

Choose Objectives and Set Strategies: To choose objectives, you simply break your short-range goals down into steps. Strategies are the actual activities that will move you toward your goals.

Let me illustrate by the following example:

If one of your short-range goals is to strengthen the relationships of the participants with their families, a good objective would be to stage two major events and 10 minor events for that purpose during the year. Your strategies might include staging a retreat for the young people where you focus on family relationships, and another one in which you invite the parents and other family members to participate in some or all of the activities. You would also develop a specific strategy for each of the minor events.

In such a scenario, you narrow down your choices of what programming materials to use on retreats, and select those materials that will enable you to move toward your goals.

Instead of wasting your opportunities on trying to come up with "something good" to do on retreats and programs, you choose objectives that will move you toward the goals you have chosen. It simplifies the selection of materials, the assignment of resources and the commitment of time and talent.

Develop Action Steps: Once you have set your objectives and strategies, develop the action steps needed to accomplish your strategies. That would include such things as:

- setting budgets
- choosing materials
- assigning people
- selecting sites
- promoting
- providing transportation (if needed)
- handling the myriads of necessary details

In this step you decide exactly what actions have to take place to make each event a success. This way, you know in advance what has to be done to make each of your programs produce the desired results.

Set Schedules: There's much more to scheduling than simply writing an event on the calendar. Good planning calls for scheduling all the action steps necessary for the success of every event.

Scheduling includes setting a deadline for every task that must be completed and assigning specific responsibility to a person for completing that task. Build in a clear-cut mechanism for reporting completion of each task — or any delay anticipated in completion — to the person responsible for overall coordination of the event.

For example, if you were scheduling a fund-raising car wash, you might want to use a four-week countdown procedure as follows:

- setting of date for car wash and location commitment (well in advance)
- appointing coordinator (well in advance) — youth director
- recruiting and training volunteers (by end of week #1) — adult coordinator
- all planning done (end of week #1) — adult coordinator
- all materials secured (end of week #1) — adult coordinator
- all promotion (started in week #2) — promotion chairperson)
- commitment of participants (end of week #3) — adult coordinator
- checking all arrangements (end of week #3) — coordinator
- final promotion (during week #4) — promotion chairperson

- implementation (on day of event) — coordinator and all volunteers

- reporting and making recommendations for future events (week after event) — coordinator

As you can see, in this sort of schedule each person knows what is expected, is equipped to do it, and has a timetable for having it done. A schedule eliminates the last-minute flurry of activity in which the youth leader runs around frantically trying to get everything done.

Interestingly, some youth directors are afraid they will offend volunteers if they tell them what to do, how to do it, and when to have it done. In all my years of experience, I have found that the opposite is true. Volunteers not only work better and accomplish more, they enjoy what they are doing a lot more when they know what to expect.

Implementation: Following Your Plan

A carefully developed plan and schedule can release you from the tension of having too much to do, and can relieve you from worrying about getting everything done on time. It can set you free to interact with other people and to enjoy your role as a youth leader.

Do What You Have Planned: If you have sought input from all people involved and have adequately planned your year of youth programming, your task is to simply carry out those plans and meet your deadlines as they come up.

But that is a very important part of organizing. I've seen some youth directors who could take a pocket calculator, a legal pad and a calendar and plan a trip to the moon. Yet, when it came time for their great launch, they couldn't get off the ground.

Here is a list of a few of the reasons that so many good plans result in failures in execution:

- The youth director wastes his time doing things that aren't on the priority list.

- The youth director fails to communicate the plans adequately to the people responsible for carrying them out.

- The youth director fails to sufficiently motivate volunteers.

- The youth director fails to secure the necessary resources to carry out the assigned tasks.

- The youth director procrastinates and allows volunteers to procrastinate until deadlines mean nothing.

- The youth director fails to follow up to see that tasks are done properly and on time.

As you can see, you as the youth director are the key person in executing the plan that has been set up. If you adequately do your job, most of the other people involved will get their jobs done — and enjoy doing them.

Get Yourself Organized: Just for fun, imagine what would have happened if:

- Moses' sister had been chasing butterflies when Pharaoh's daughter came to the river to take a bath.

- David had forgotten to pick up the rocks for his slingshot.

- The disciples had been out fishing on the day of Pentecost.

You get the picture, don't you? God was able to do his part because his servants were where they should have been, doing what they should have been doing at the time God was ready to act.

There is nothing "unspiritual" about being organized. In fact, good stewardship calls for being organized — both personally and in all we do.

Here are some tips on getting organized:

1. ***Use a daily "to do list."*** Write down all the things scheduled on your calendar, and any other things you know you must do. Then, rank the list by priorities and start at the top. As you complete each task, mark it off and move to the next. That way, you will get more done in less time, and you will always know what to do next.

2. ***Get started right each day.*** Set your alarm for exactly the time you should arise, and get up as soon as it goes off. Lay out your clothes each night before you go to bed. Know at least the first three things you should do in the morning — before you retire at night.

3. ***Handle details; don't shuffle paperwork.*** There is no value in looking at a letter or memo half a dozen times. Make a decision, act and file the paper.

4. ***Unclutter your life.*** An efficiency expert can tell more about you than a handwriting expert can — by simply looking at the top of your desk. Effective youth workers keep every area of their lives uncluttered and ready for action.

5. ***Put off procrastination.*** Putting things off is a nasty habit that robs you of the precious moments you need to do a good job. If something is worth doing, it is worth doing at the appointed time. Cultivate the habit of doing things as they come up.

6. ***Practice time management.*** Cultivate the habit of using every moment available to work on your goals. Work when you work, and play when it's time to play. But don't mix the two.

7. ***Always have something constructive to do.*** Unnecessary delays come along in everyone's life. When you're stuck in traffic, or waiting to see someone, it's a good time to catch up on some of the little tasks on your schedule.

Communicate Effectively with Volunteers

Effective leaders leave nothing to chance. They don't assume that a volunteer knows what to do, and how to do it. They make sure that volunteer knows what to do and when and how to do it.

Equipping, training and directing volunteers is such an important part of organizing that I will devote a chapter to it later. Right now, let me simply observe that nothing you have written down on a calendar or a piece of paper is of any value until it is effectively communicated to the volunteer you want to do it.

Communicate Effectively with Youth and Their Parents

If you've spent weeks planning wonderful things for the youth in your group, by all means let them in on what you're planning for them to do.

- *Inform* them as to what is coming up and how they can fit into it.

- *Motivate* them to participate in each activity.

- *Build excitement and enthusiasm* for all upcoming events.

- *Listen* to their feedback to make sure they understand and are as enthusiastic about your plans as you are.

- *Guide* them step by step as to what you want them to do.

- *Correct* their misconceptions of what you expect.

- *Check* to see that they are doing what you expect.

- *Encourage* them to invite others to participate with them.

- *Stimulate* them to actively participate.

- *Make sure* their parents know what to expect and what you want them to do.

Monitoring: Your Thermostat

Do you know the difference between a thermometer and a thermostat? A thermometer only tells you the temperature in your environment, but a thermostat triggers a change in that environment. A thermostat can turn on a heater if the temperature is too low, or it can set off an air conditioner if the temperature is too high.

Worry is a thermometer. That nagging feeling that something is not getting done, that frantic rushing around trying to get overdue things done, and blaming someone for not doing a task: these are all like the thermometer. They make you uptight and irritable, but do little to really solve problems.

But monitoring is a thermostat. When you have built monitoring mechanisms into your plans, they almost automatically trigger actions that will correct problems and delays that arise. Monitoring is one of the most liberating techniques I have found — both in my personal life and in youth work.

It's as simple as scheduling all the little events that have to take place to make a big event happen when and in the ways you want it to happen, then checking regularly to see that all those little events take place.

Jesus — the Master Monitor: "It was before the Passover festival. Jesus knew that his hour had come and he must leave the world and go to the Father." (John 13:1)

The greatest event in history was about to take place — the death of our Lord on the cross. And it was right on schedule! Nowhere in history can you find a greater example of planning, implementation and monitoring than that reflected in the four Gospels.

Consider how many "little" events had to occur along the way to set the stage for the crucifixion and resurrection. Here are only a few that serve to illustrate the point:

- the miraculous birth of Jesus in Bethlehem

- the silent years of growing up in Nazareth

- the teaching event in Jerusalem, at the age of 12

- the first year of public ministry — often called the "year of obscurity"

- the second year, known as the "year of public favor"

- the third year, sometimes called the "year of opposition"

- the triumphal entry into Jerusalem

- the "passion week"

- the Last Supper

- the arrest and trial

These represent only a few of the events along the way to God's redemptive act on the cross. Within each of those events, there were many "minor" events that happened by divine plan, and right on schedule.

As I have read the Bible, I have been constantly amazed at how deliberately Jesus did everything. There is no evidence that he ever was in a state of panic, or that he rushed around in confusion, or that he ever wondered what to do next.

If Jesus was our great example, then it seems to me there is never any excuse for sloppily organizing our efforts to communicate his Gospel to the young people he loves.

A Practical Plan of Monitoring: It has only been within the last century that modern man has discovered the value and simplicity that God used "before the foundation of the world."

Most giant factories and large organizations now use a system called CPM/PERT to enable them to build huge airplanes, computers and automobiles, or to send men to the moon.

CPM/PERT is a complicated sounding name for a very simple process that can take the confusion out of organizing almost anything — including a youth program, a weekend retreat or a Christmas program. The initials stand for "Critical Path Method/Project Evaluation and Review Technique."

Whether you use a million-dollar computer or a simple desk calendar, "Critical Path Method" means that you set a target date for accomplishing each task along the way to reaching the goal you have set.

For example, if you determine that it will take 12 weeks to plan and implement a weekend retreat, you list all the things that must happen in each of the 12 weeks. The success of the retreat is assured by the things that get done during the first week, and the second week — right on through the 12th week.

By laying it all out before you, you and all the people working with you know how to work together. The person responsible for buying the food knows how many people to buy for soon enough to buy the right quantities; the promotion chairperson knows what the programming will be so that printed materials can be prepared; and the transportation chairperson knows well in advance what the needs and costs will be. We will see how important it is for everyone to understand what is expected of them in our chapter on working with volunteers.

Now here's where monitoring comes into the picture. "Project Evaluation and Review Technique" means that you set up — in advance — a system for making sure that everything happens when it is scheduled to happen.

If a scheduled event doesn't take place, then you know it immediately and you can readily see how that missed deadline is going to affect the whole project. By seeing the delay early enough, you can make whatever adjustments you need to make to compensate.

For example, if you know it will take three weeks to get the printing of a brochure done, and the promotion chairperson is a week late getting the copy ready, you know that it will have an effect on every other part of the schedule.

Monitoring Mechanisms: There are several useful tools you can build into your planning for successful programming. When these are operating correctly, they are like alarms that go off when some adjustment is needed.

1. **Countdown calendar:** Most office supply stores carry large planning calendars that can be very useful in monitoring. They come in large desk-top models, wall-hanging models, and in book form. Use whichever form works best for you.

   Make sure that the calendar you buy has plenty of space for you to write down all the deadlines in your planning schedule. As deadlines are met, they can be checked off. When they are not met, the countdown calendar gives you a panoramic view of the project so that you can reschedule other deadlines to adjust for the delays.

2. **Tickler file:** Many youth directors find a tickler file helpful in staying abreast of their deadlines. Such a file can be particularly useful when you have the availability of a secretary.

   The idea is to file specific things you — or someone else — should be doing in order to meet a deadline, in a file set up by dates. For example, your card for a certain date might read as follows:

   DATE: November 1

   Call Mary Smith re promotional brochure copy (deadline 11/5).

   Call Joe Doe re banquet menu (deadline 11/5).

   Call Bill Jones re door prizes (deadline 11/10).

   Meet with the minister re spring retreat planning schedule (deadline 12/31).

   The tickler file alerts you as to what you should be doing, and what you should be reminding others to do.

3. **Progress reports:** As you are communicating assignments to all the people involved in a program or project, build in a scheduled reporting date for each stage of progress. This will let the person know that the task is important and give you a simple mechanism for keeping abreast of what is going on.

4. **Organizational meetings:** Some youth directors prefer to handle everything by telephone, but others

prefer to hold scheduled report meetings where all phases of a project are updated. The advantage of the telephone approach is that it can save time for those involved.

However, there a couple of strong advantages to holding report meetings. First, it helps to keep everybody enthused and feeling like part of a team. Second, when adjustments are necessary, the whole schedule can be changed and all people notified without a lot of follow-up on your part. This can be particularly helpful if there are widely differing opinions on how things should be done. It can save you from getting caught in the middle.

Even if you use the meeting approach, it might be helpful to touch bases with key people before the meeting to make sure that all items that need attention get put onto the agenda.

Nothing Works Unless You Do

There's an old line from Scottish literature about the "best-laid plans 'o men and mice" going astray. Sometimes, despite all you can do, your best organization efforts will fail.

When that happens, the most important thing to do is to determine exactly what went wrong, why it went wrong, and how it can be avoided in future efforts.

Since I will have much more to say about that in the chapter on evaluating, let me simply point out here that the single greatest cause of organizational failure is that somebody fails to fulfill his or her responsibilities. Unfortunately, the someone is most often the leader.

Remember: *Nothing works unless you do!* It is an exciting thing to see the carefully laid plan literally spring from the countdown calendar and become action that results in young people finding and growing in Christ. That only happens when you follow through with all the details you have scheduled.

Two Major Enemies

There are two major enemies that constantly attack your efforts to work your plan.

Diversion of your energies is the first major enemy. There will always be so many opportunities to do good things and urgent things that you will have to fight valiantly to stick to the plans you have laid.

Many youth directors concentrate on activities, but effective youth directors concentrate all their energies on working the plans they have laid. They consider any opportunity to spend time pursuing unscheduled activities to be diversions, and only take part in them if they have extra time.

Procrastination is the other major enemy to your efforts to work your plan. When a deadline comes up, there is often the temptation to delay it until a later time. As you succumb to the procrastination habit, your schedule becomes a burden rather than an asset to you.

There are several reasons we tend to procrastinate:

- We think the task will be easier or more pleasant later.

- We simply don't feel like doing the task.

- We kid ourselves into thinking we will have more time later.

- We develop the habit of procrastinating in everything.

The best weapon against procrastination is loyalty to the goals we have set and the plans we have made to enable us to reach those goals. If we can keep those goals in focus, and consider the deadlines we set as almost sacred, we can avoid the nasty habit of putting things off.

GROWTH EXERCISE

Take a project of your choosing and, using the stages of organizing outlined in this chapter, work a complete plan for implementation.

CHAPTER 11

How to Work Effectively with Volunteers

If you were given the task of changing the course of the history of the world, and you were only given three years to do it, how would you go about it? That is precisely the task that Jesus was given and almost exactly the amount of time allocated for him to do it. The Bible tells us that Jesus chose to do it working through other people. He chose 12 disciples.

The 12 people he chose were about as unlikely a bunch as you would find working as volunteers in many youth programs in churches throughout America. However, make no mistake about it, they were carefully chosen by Jesus and they were chosen to fulfill specific roles in the establishment of the church and the spreading of the Gospel.

Those who were chosen went through an intensive training and growth process for three years, and when the time came they were ready to perform the tasks Jesus left for them to do in the face of the worst persecution we could ever imagine. They were even prepared to lay down their lives for him. Tradition tells us that is exactly what most of them did. Of the 11 disciples who remained true to Jesus, 10 died martyr's deaths. The only one who escaped was John, and he escaped from a vat of boiling oil because God wanted him to write "The Revelation." A careful study of the New Testament reveals that the master plan of evangelism is that God chooses to work through people to reach other people with the good news of the Gospel. With Jesus as our great example, let's look more carefully at the task of working through volunteers to carry on youth ministry in the local church.

Recruiting, training and supervising the activities of volunteer workers is one of the greatest challenges faced by the youth leader today. Those who give it its proper priority and work at it with patience reap rich rewards and success; they are able to provide great benefits for the young people in their group. Those who choose to work as Lone Rangers tend to work themselves to death with minimal results.

Enlisting the aid of volunteers can be a very frustrating task because they often appear preoccupied with their own lives or only mildly interested in working with young people, sometimes demonstrate a marked lack of ability, and occasionally are very uncooperative.

It is a painful experience for a youth leader to invest hours and hours in planning and implementing an important project only to have it messed up by incompetent and uncaring volunteers. The risk is always that volunteers may fail in their attempts to do very important tasks.

A Team Effort

Most people readily recall that dramatic chariot race in the movie *Ben Hur*. However, there is a scene just before that which is equally dramatic — though not as spectacular.

Young Judah is working with five Arabian stallions and is thoroughly frustrated because he can't get them to work together. When he snaps the whip, they all pull in different directions: one or two of them will balk and refuse to move, and they all appear frightened.

Suddenly an old Bedoin horse trainer steps onto the scene. Judah knows that the upcoming chariot race is the most important event of his life, and expresses the anxiety he feels because he knows his team is simply not ready for the challenge. The old man offers his help, which the young chariot racer readily accepts.

With a look of love in his eyes, this experienced horse trainer walks to the front of the animals and remarks, "They are beautiful babies!" Quietly, he pats each one on the nose and speaks softly to them.

He then addresses the task of correcting problems with their harnesses. "They are not working together as a team," he says as he tightens a strap here and loosens a strap there and adjusts a collar. After carefully adjusting the entire harness, he climbs into the chariot, gives a strong, clear command and instantly five horses move out as one.

A quick turn around the track, and the old trainer smilingly hands the reins to young Judah with the statement, "They must work together as one!"

When the day of the great race comes, they are ready and equal to the challenge. It is obvious as you watch them on the screen that the problem was not with the horses. The problem was with the man, who did not understand the principles of getting them prepared and willing to work together with each other and with him.

In your attempts to minister to youth you will find that there are many young people and adults who are willing, able and sometimes even eager to work with you in fulfilling your ministry; but your task is to get them to work together as a team. This can only happen when you carefully select them for the specific tasks you have in mind, thoroughly train and equip them to do the job and direct their activities with love and gentle firmness.

The "KIS/MIF" Principle

The most important principle in working with volunteers — both youth and adults — is expressed by the acronym KIS/MIF. That translates as: "Keep It Simple/Make It Fun."

You will be tempted to judge the commitment level and capabilities of volunteers by your own, but volunteers seldom perform at the level of the people who have the primary responsibility for a program.

Keep it simple! Peter Drucker, who has so much to say about management, says that the most important principle in working with other people is to break down tasks into "manageable functions that people can easily do."

Many studies have been done in recent years on the reasons behind "volunteer burnout." The Development Association for Christian Institutes suggests that there are basically eight reasons people refuse to volunteer again after dropping out from working in the church or other organizations. The reasons are explained by volunteers' comments:

- "They didn't explain the job or how to go about it."
- "They expected too much."
- "They didn't provide leadership along the way."
- "They never gave me any tools to work with."
- "They forgot about me after they gave me the job."
- "They were so disorganized that I really couldn't get my job done."
- "They didn't seem very enthusiastic or appreciative of the job I did."
- "I told them I didn't know anything about that job, and couldn't do it, but they insisted."

As you can see from the list, volunteers are often frustrated because the leader did not "keep it simple." Volunteers can do amazing things when they are properly directed and challenged by an effective youth leader. This sign appears on the wall of one of the most effective leaders I have ever known: "We the unwilling, led by the unqualified, have been doing the unbelievable for so long, with so little, that we now attempt the impossible with nothing!"

Make it fun! I have seen young people who wouldn't lift a finger to clean up their own rooms at home spend a full day at a time doing some of the grubbiest work you can imagine, cleaning up an old building for a church. The secret? Somebody made it fun.

Here are some pointers on how to make any task fun for volunteers:

1. ***People enjoy doing things together.***

2. ***People enjoy a sense of accomplishment.*** They prefer to start with small tasks they know they can easily accomplish before they move on to more complicated tasks.

3. ***People need "stroking."*** Someone who has had a bad day or is simply feeling down can be encouraged by a gentle word from an understanding, caring leader who knows what that person is investing in that attempt to help.

4. ***People like to be recognized for their achievements.*** A sincere compliment, a pat on the back in front of the group or some tangible form of recognition can go a long way in helping a volunteer enjoy working with the young people in your church.

5. ***Criticize very sparingly and never in public.*** No one likes to be embarrassed or humiliated in the presence of other people. The secret to criticism is to make the person feel that you are attempting to help him be more effective at something in which you know him to be interested.

6. ***Be tactful.*** Ask people to do things, don't order them around. Remember, they are volunteers and need to be encouraged, not commanded, to do things.

7. ***Be cheerful.*** There is no place for moodiness in leading volunteers. Even the most frustrating, tension-causing circumstances can be made fun by a cheerful leader who can see the humor in a situation, laugh about it and enable other people to laugh.

8. *Be enthusiastic.* People enjoy doing what matters to them. The best was to make something matter to another person is to convince him by your attitude that it matters a great deal to you.

9. *Keep it moving.* People have fun doing things that are organized and flow smoothly. They tend to become discouraged when they feel their time is being wasted.

10. *Take each person seriously.* People enjoy hearing their names called, they enjoy talking, and they enjoy feeling that they matter a great deal to you.

The youth leader who learns to live by the KIS/MIF Principle will have little difficulty recruiting and keeping volunteers. Someone has defined work as "doing something you don't like to do." If you will always keep it simple and make it fun, you will find that volunteers relate to it as play and not work.

Identifying Potential Volunteers

Of all the tasks that vie for your attention, none is more important than the cultivation of volunteer workers — both adult and youth — to assist you in the day-to-day running of your church's youth ministry. Pick them well, facilitate their effectiveness, and maintain constant and open communication with them. Many people within the church who have great leadership and volunteer potential are overlooked simply because the youth leader fails to recognize their commitment and abilities.

The following is a list of things you might look for in trying to spot leadership capabilities:

1. *A good volunteer must have love and concern for people* — especially youth. The single most important ingredient of any youth ministry is love. Anyone who really loves young people can be equipped for some kind of volunteer work.

2. *A strong Christian commitment is necessary* if a person is to be an effective leader of your church's youth. If he has all the other capabilities listed here but lacks the Christian commitment, he should not be put into a leadership role until that commitment has been cultivated.

3. *Spiritual and emotional maturity* are also important elements of volunteer leadership. There are many

pressures in working with young people, and someone who comes apart under stress cannot function effectively in a leadership role. A good sense of humor helps, too.

4. *A good leader must have a well-developed sense of responsibility and a willingness to follow through* with what he commits himself to do. Many young people interpret a lack of responsibility as rejection, and someone who operates irresponsibly in your church's name can do a lot of damage.

5. *A good relationship with one's family is a tremendous asset.* This is particularly important if you plan to place a strong emphasis on ministry to the family as a unit.

6. *Leadership involves setting a good example.* In areas that your church considers important, does the person you are considering for a leadership role provide a good example for the young people to emulate?

7. *Look for people who demonstrate an ability to get along well with others.* Remember, as a youth leader, you are attempting to build a team. You certainly don't need an individual who is hard to get along with and who will constantly disrupt your activities.

8. *Stay alert for special talents displayed by church members.* Someone who has abilities in art, photography, music, organizing or any other such skill can be a tremendous asset to your ministry.

9. *Look for people who are busy.* It is an old adage, but a great truth: "If you want something done, ask a busy person to do it." Those who have abilities which they willingly use usually find plenty of work to do — but if they are interested and motivated, they will assist you in your task as a youth leader.

10. *Ask other volunteers to help you with spotting leadership capabilities.* This is particularly important in a large church or organization. In a church that has hundreds of members it is quite possible that you will overlook people who have great potential but who are not assertive in expressing that potential. By asking others to assist you, you will be able to uncover valuable talents that might otherwise be missed.

How to Recruit Workers

A youth leader who says, "People aren't interested in working with the young people in our church," is only admitting failure in recruiting attempts. When people are properly approached, asked to do tasks that they feel comfortable doing, and are sold on the importance of those tasks, they will respond unless they are so obligated otherwise that they simply have no time.

Here are some tips that can help you increase your "batting average" in recruiting workers:

1. *People do things for their reasons, not yours.* Recognize that you are not asking a person to do you a favor. As a youth leader you are giving that person an opportunity to engage in one of the Christian church's most exciting pursuits. You cannot consistently make people do things they do not want to do; you can only invite them to do things that they feel are important.

2. *Always seek to match the person's interest and capabilities to the leadership role you are inviting him to fulfill.* People usually enjoy doing things they do well, and they usually do them better than anyone else could do them.

3. *Approach a potential volunteer well in advance and prepare him for the possibility that he will be asked more specifically later.* Some of the best leaders in the local church commit themselves at least a year in advance. You are, to some extent, in competition with other activities that vie for their time.

4. *Assure all prospective volunteers that they will be trained and equipped* for the task you are asking them to do. Many *no* answers could be turned into *yes* if the workers felt confident that training and equipping would be available before the time the task is to be performed.

5. *Always be as specific as possible about what you want the person to do.* In fact, it is helpful to take a written job description for the person to consider. When you ask someone to do something in a general way, when they get around to it, it is doubtful that it will ever be done and almost certain that it will not be done well.

6. *Assure the person that you are asking for a firm decision,* and if necessary allow him to take time to think and pray about it before giving you an answer. Never assume that a person who gives you a tentative commitment will come through when it's time.

7. *Consider yourself to be a salesperson when you are recruiting a volunteer.* It has been proven that people do not back good causes or take on volunteer tasks because "it's their responsibility." They respond to invitations to do things that they are convinced are worth the time and effort they will put into them. Always make your appeal to the person's interests and strengths when you are assigning a task.

8. *Always appeal to people on an individual basis.* If possible, make an appointment to see the person. Sit down and make the presentation as if you feel it is important, and that person is important. It is sometimes helpful to take a young person with you when you go to make your appeal for the volunteer to get involved.

9. *Never overburden a willing volunteer.* Youth leaders often fail to recruit enough workers to carry on the responsibilities of youth ministry, and therefore must rely on the few who are willing to work to carry the full load. Assure any prospective volunteer that you are asking for a commitment for a specific amount of time, and only for that amount of time — then stick by your commitment.

10. *After the volunteer has made a commitment, make sure you provide a steady stream of information* to him so his interest will be constantly increasing until you are ready for him to serve. That way, not only will he feel you are interested, but he will build enthusiasm and be ready when it's time to go.

These are simple tips, but you would be surprised how many youth leaders ignore some of the basic principles I have presented in trying to recruit workers. Remember, it is your task to recruit workers. To say there are not enough workers is only to admit that you have failed to do your job as a leader.

Special note: Jesus made it quite clear that we are to pray for the Lord to send "workers unto the harvest." Successful youth leaders usually spend a great deal of time in prayer that God will direct them to those people who need to serve, who can serve, and who want to serve.

How to Train Workers

We have talked about the need to train workers. Now let's turn our attention to the subject of how to train workers.

Training can be viewed from three different perspectives: initial training, ongoing training and motivation. All three types of training are useful, but the degree to which you will use each depends on the workers' needs, the complexity of the project you are asking them to undertake, and the amount of time they will be required to commit.

Workshops and Seminars

Probably the most effective way of training a large group of workers at one time is the workshop or seminar. Seminars are basically sessions held to disseminate information, motivate workers and obtain a desired response.

If your program is rather complex and you will be involving many workers, you may need to hold several workshops. A weekend retreat with the workers might create the kind of atmosphere in which you can cover all the ground you need to cover without saturating their minds with information.

Two hours is about the maximum timespan for a workshop. Beyond that, bodies and minds become tired and restless.

Setting the stage for a workshop is important. First, make it clear to all who will attend what time you expect to start and that they will miss something very important if they are late. Make it equally clear that the plan is for a workshop and not a play session. While the atmosphere should be comfortable, it ought not be conducive to too much relaxation. Everyone needs to know that he is there for a specific purpose, and that you are approaching it as if it is the most important thing in the world for you at that time.

How to Hold a Workshop

1. *Make sure that everyone understands where and when the workshop will be held and that you plan to start on time.*

2. *Gather all the materials you will need for the workshop:*

- All programming materials and supporting information

- A study guide for the workshop itself

- A chalkboard, chalk and eraser

- A cassette and cassette player if you plan to use one in this seminar

- Make sure the room is ready and will be comfortable.

3. *Make the necessary personal preparation.*

- Make sure that you understand the purpose of this workshop and know what you hope to accomplish. It may be helpful for you to try to boil down the whole workshop into one sentence that clearly covers your whole objective.

- Study in depth all the materials that you plan to cover.

- After all materials are assembled and you are familiar with everything, go through a dummy run to make sure you are ready and nothing is missing.

Workshop Procedure

1. *Start on time and get right down to business.*

- Assure group members that you respect their time and will try to close at exactly the appointed hour. Ask for their cooperation so that all the material may be covered.

- Tell them that there will be appropriate times during the workshop for questions and discussion. Ask them to hold all questions and comments until the allotted times.

2. *Follow specific steps.*

- Start with prayer. The prayer should not be a general rambling prayer that covers the whole world. It should be brief, to the point, and specifically related to the meeting you are now conducting.

- Give out the study guides you have developed. Make sure that each participant has one. Indicate that you will be covering everything contained in the study guides and that they do not need to be read all the way through before you get started.

- Give a brief talk on the importance of the task the volunteer workers are to do. You may want to use the chalkboard to further emphasize your points.

- Cover all the material and program strategies to be used. Make sure they are covered in sufficient detail such that everyone understands them.

- Ask for feedback and questions so you can determine that everyone understands what you are trying to accomplish through the program. If you sense negative feelings in one or two people toward the program, assure them that you will be happy to discuss more details with them after the workshop. Try to deal constructively with feelings that people have, but don't get bogged down.

- Give each worker a specific job description. Ask the workers to look over the job descriptions, and try to answer any questions. Make sure they understand that a part of their job is to provide feedback and monitoring information to you.

- Talk to the group about being enthusiastic and approaching the job with confidence. Some points you might want to cover are:

    ▪ Always be excited. Young people are not as likely to get as excited as the workers but almost certainly they will be no more excited about programs than are their leaders.

- Always be prepared. If this motto is good enough for the scouts, it is good enough for your workers.

- Assure them that they can do the job with God's help.

- Assure them that you and the other church staff members support them and stand ready to help at any time.

- Encourage them to seek the anointing of the Holy Spirit before every endeavor with young people.

● Adjourn and have fellowship. During this time, you ought to move around and talk to as many people as possible, keeping an ear open for feelings that indicate a need for follow-up. If someone is uncomfortable with a job or does not understand the program, these feelings could come out in a casual fellowship time after adjournment.

On-the-Job Training

The workshop is good for getting things started, but it will not solve all your problems. Your workers need on-the-job training on a weekly basis.

Some guidelines for ongoing training are:

1. *Constantly seek to motivate and inspire the workers.* Remember, they are out there where it's rough and need all the help they can get.

2. *Constantly feed them information* that will help them understand young people, help them do a better job, and give them inspiration and hope.

3. *Monitor regularly their successes and failures.* Rejoice with them in successes and join with them in concern over their frustrations.

4. *Make them feel important—they are important.*

   ● Ask for their opinions.

- Give them a voice in all planning for the future.

- Give public recognition to all your workers at every opportunity.

- Fight the feeling of isolation by showing that each worker is part of the total team. Make workers aware that their problems are everybody's problems. Also, share some good times with them.

How to Supervise Volunteers

A friend of mine tells the following story which I think illustrates very clearly the most important principle of leading volunteers:

"When I was a little boy I often visited my grandmother, who had a large flock of chickens. On one such visit she invited me to put the chickens into their house for safekeeping for the night. Excitedly, I accepted the invitation.

"I went out into the chickenyard and started attempting to herd the chickens into the tiny door of the chickenhouse. They started squawking and running in all different directions, and after 15 minutes of frantically running around, I had not been able to get one chicken into that coop.

"My grandmother stood watching the procedure and chuckling. 'Do you need some help?' she asked.

" 'These chickens just will not go into that chickenhouse!' I said, showing my frustration.

"I watched as my grandmother walked over and picked up a bucket of feed and began making clucking noises. Soon every chicken in that yard was standing at her feet. Quietly talking to them, she began to walk toward the door of the chickenhouse. Soon all the chickens were in the house and locked up securely for the night.

"She then fed them from the bucket so that they would continue to trust her in the future.

"I learned that day that it is a lot easier to lead chickens than it is to drive them."

Any youth leader who has attempted to coordinate the efforts of a large group of volunteers while keeping up with an even larger group of young people knows that in at least one respect, people can be a lot like chickens. They are much easier to lead through incentives than they are to drive or force to do the things you want them to do.

See Their Point of View

Volunteers were once asked to describe what they expected from a youth leader in supervising their activities and motivating them to do the tasks that lay ahead for them. The following is a list they made:

- Stand by us, not over us. Give us the feeling that we are not alone in the world, that we can always count on you when we are in trouble.

- Make us feel that we are loved and wanted.

- Train us by being affectionately firm. You will achieve more through patient teaching than by criticism or preaching.

- Disagree with us when you feel it is necessary, but explain why you are disagreeing.

- Equip us so that we will not always need you. Teach us how to take on responsibility and become independent of you.

- Don't act shocked when we fail to do things you feel we should do. It is going to take us some time to learn how to carry our responsibility properly.

- Try to be as consistent as possible. If you are confused about what you want from us, why shouldn't we be confused, too, in what we give you?

- Don't try to make us feel inferior. We have enough self-doubts without your confirming those doubts. Predicting failure for us won't help us succeed.

GROWTH EXERCISE

List at least three projects to which you have given a con-siderable amount of your time as a volunteer and answer the following questions about each:

1. **Why did you become involved in the project?**

2. **How did the leader go about recruiting you for the task?**

3. **What kind of training did you receive to help you adequately do the job?**

4. **Do you feel that the leader of the project could have been more helpful to you in carrying out the task to which you were assigned? If so, how?**

CHAPTER 12

Principles of Creative Programming

Ever wonder why some youth activities are full of life, with many young people excitedly participating, while other groups struggle along with the young people looking as if they're about to fall asleep?

The first group is probably led by a person who understands the principles of *involvement*.

Levels of Involvement

There are three basic levels at which people become involved in program activities. The amount of learning, growing and enthusiasm will usually be determined by the level of involvement.

- level one: What I hear, I forget.

- level two: What I see, I remember.

- level three: What I do, I understand.

That list implies a rule which effective youth leaders rely heavily upon: "I will never tell a person anything I can better show, and I will never simply show a person anything that I can let the person do."

What Is Creative Programming?

"I'm not a very creative person," I have heard many youth leaders claim at seminars I have conducted.

I believe that every person alive has the potential of being creative. It may be true that there are some people who have a natural curiosity and inventiveness that enables them to be more innovative, but all of us can create. Creativity is a God-given ability. The Bible tells us that we are made in the image of God. If we can claim our heritage, and let our minds roam freely, most of us will be surprised at how creative we can be.

There are several hindrances to creativity. Check below to see if any of the ones listed block you and keep you from being as creative as you would like to be:

- *Laziness:* Creativity involves thinking and doing. Some people would rather be told what to do.

- *Fear of the unknown:* There is always the risk of failure in trying new ideas and methods. Many would rather do it the old way.

- *Timidity:* A new idea or program might not work, and many people fear that they will be embarrassed if everyone doesn't respond favorably.

- *Lack of commitment:* Creativity takes thought, effort and time. If you are not committed to what you're doing, it is easier to just slop through every activity.

- *A negative attitude:* Some people see only the problems, while others get excited about the opportunities. The optimist finds ways to get things done.

If you would become more creative, let your mind run free, let your spirit soar, let your dreams take tangible form. The people in your youth group will love it. And they probably will pick up the rhythm of your new approach and stimulate you to be even more creative. Creative programming is attempting new things for God, and trying new ways of doing things that have become ineffective.

The Greatest Source of Creativity

Young minds are usually the greatest source of creativity. They have not yet learned all the reasons why things can't be done; they are willing to reach out to test the untried; and they are alert to new information.

The creative minds of the youth in your group provide a think tank and idea bank for solving problems, finding and developing new approaches, and capitalizing on new opportunities. Some of the most effective youth ministries I have ever seen are built around ideas the young people themselves present and develop. That doesn't happen automatically. It results from careful cultivation of creativity by an effective youth leader.

Here are some ways you can cultivate the creativity in your group:

1. ***Be a catalyst:*** Remember that people learn best by doing. Maintain a creative atmosphere where the young people are encouraged to contribute new ideas and try new experiences. Don't be afraid the youth will get out of hand. The opposite is usually true — when their ideas are respected and their talents fully utilized, they will control the group for you.

2. ***Be a facilitator:*** People learn most readily what is significant to them as individuals. One of the oldest tricks in the book is to give a troublemaker a useful task to perform, or assign a problem that affects the whole group to someone who refuses to get involved. Suddenly the person gets involved with the group and everybody benefits.

3. ***Be an enabler:*** If people learn and grow best by doing, look for every way possible to enable them to experience new adventures. Keep in mind that people need to experience small victories first, then move on to bigger and better things. When the youth in your group come to look upon you as a resource person who enables them to do things that matter to them, they will respect you as a valuable friend.

4. ***Be a stimulator:*** Many are timid; some are lazy; some are afraid they will fail. Stimulate them to act by holding out incentives and giving praise for their accomplishments. Raise questions that cause them to think things through for themselves. It is better for people to discover what matters to them than it is for you to tell them.

5. ***Be an encourager:*** "You can do it! I'll help you!" is one of the most valuable expressions a youth leader can learn. One of the most encouraging things you can do is to be willing to make a fool of yourself in front of the group. When people learn that it is no big deal to make a mistake, they will gain new courage to try things themselves.

6. ***Be a discoverer:*** You don't have to know everything to be an effective youth leader. In fact, if you participate in the learning process, you become a fellow traveler with others in the group. As they see the joy you receive from trying new things and making new discoveries, they will join with you.

Creative youth programming is almost always a group effort. The more you can get the young people and the adult volunteers involved in the development of programs and projects, the more creative those things will be.

The Church as a Learning/ Growth Center

One of the most exciting concepts of the gospel of Christ is that he can change lives. As young people assimilate the teachings of Christ into the daily experiences of their lives, they are changed for the better. It's all a part of the process of redemption.

The best test of how effective a youth ministry is, is the test of how great an impact it has on the attitudes and actions of the people in the group. As people grow in their relationships with God, they change the way they live.

Thus, the church becomes a learning center, a place where growth takes place. This process suggests several important considerations in the operation of an effective youth program.

Learning Centers Are Places Equipped for Growth

Whether the available space is a small room or a large educational building, it is helpful to think of it as a learning/growth center. Start where you are with what is available, and create an atmosphere that stimulates personal growth and development.

Every wall can become a bulletin board for displaying teaching, stimulating and informing materials. I've seen some rooms in churches that were so excitingly updated each week that the young people would come early for a peek at what new things were posted.

Learning Centers Have a Purpose and a Plan

What distinguishes a learning center from an interest center or a casual environment is that it has a set purpose, a direction, a carefully planned theme. That theme might change from week to week, but it always moves in a certain direction; it is always targeted at a specific goal.

The producers of television commercials know that they have only 30 seconds to get across their message, so they design every element of that commercial to perform a specific function. It is not at all unusual for a large company to spend $200,000 filming one commercial, because they want to make it count.

Likewise, we have access to young people for only a short time each week. We need to invest every effort and resource possible to use that time to maximum advantage.

Learning Centers Have Instructions

The best collection of learning materials, equipment and themes are of little value unless the young people know how to take advantage of the treasures they offer. Translating the purpose or learning goal of a presentation into tangible activities that young people can understand is often a great challenge, but it is extremely important.

The better the planning and the more thorough the instructions, the better the young people can participate without adult supervision.

Learning Centers Operate with Resource People

"You can't answer questions nobody is asking" is an old saying, but it is still very true. When group leaders are viewed as instructors, they tend to give out the information they want to convey, and often fail to answer the important questions young people are asking.

In the learning center, the adults become resource people who can help young people make discoveries for themselves. They seek to inspire young people to search. Instead of answering questions, they become masters at asking questions and creating curiosity within the youngsters.

"Why do you always answer every question I ask with another question?" asked a young person of such a resource person.

Learning Centers Have Resource Materials

Many church bodies find it helpful to create various material centers where the young people can find resources to facilitate learning. They might include:

- *A biblical resource center:* Bibles, Bible story books, concordances, maps, Bible dictionaries and commentaries could be included.

- *A music center:* This would provide songbooks, sheet

music, records, tapes, cassettes, instruments, etc.

- *A media center:* This is often equipped with television, radio, cassette players, videocassette players, magazines and newspapers.

- *A project supplies center:* All kinds of art supplies, writing materials, skit props and other materials can be provided.

The idea of the centers is to provide materials that fit the curriculum of the learning center and the needs of the young people. Rules for usage should be clearly stated and strongly enforced, but not so restrictive as to crush creativity.

Using Multimedia

Today's young people have grown up in a media-saturated world. At home they watch television, play video games, listen to radios and stereos, and play with personal computers. In school and recreational facilities they see movies, learn through complex media centers, and see concerts with full light shows.

As a result, they have become very conscious of multimedia stimulation. This awareness presents several problems for the youth leader who would communicate with them:

- They get bored easily and tend to have short attention spans.

- They tune out any input they don't want to receive.

- They are drawn to secular media they find more attractive.

- They find it more comfortable to be spectators than participants.

"If you can't beat 'em, join 'em!" That old saying holds a valuable clue as to what to do about the problems presented by all the media exposure.

Understand Media

Some youth leaders are frightened at the prospect of getting involved with multimedia communication because they think it is too complicated. What many of them don't realize is that they are already involved with multimedia in their programming. They have only to expand what they are doing to become more effective.

A medium is nothing more than a tool that enables you to convey a message more effectively. For example, if you are lecturing and you hold up a picture that illustrates a point, that's a medium. (*Media* is the plural form of *medium.*)

If you use two or more media, you have entered the world of multimedia. For example, if you turn the pages of a flip chart while you are playing a prerecorded tape, you've got multimedia.

Multimedia can be as simple as a pointing stick with a chart, or as complicated as a mind-boggling, sense-overloading audiovisual presentation. The level of usage depends on the resources you have available, your knowledge of available resources, the complexity of the subject, and the time you have to prepare. A good rule of thumb is: *Always look for the most effective way available to present an idea.*

Go Visual

Television has become the eye to the world for the typical young person. He is accustomed to seeing everything in "living color."

Visuals are effective in teaching and motivating young people because:

- They convey messages to the most highly developed sense — seeing.
- They concentrate interest and attention.
- They can relate abstract principles to concrete objects.
- They can clearly illustrate relationships.
- They can convey instantly messages that are too complex to put into words.
- They reinforce the message, again and again.

Some of the most effective visuals I have ever seen were simple to produce and cost little or nothing. Here are some ideas for simple, low-cost visuals:

Use Bulletin Boards

I recently spoke at a church that was alive with beautifully done bulletin boards. They added so much that I asked the youth director to tell me her secret for making them so effective. Here are some tips she gave me:

- Keep them simple enough that the viewer can get the message at a glance.

- Make them interesting by using images with which young people are familiar.

- Make them colorful.

- Create a feeling of motion in the images.

- Change them often.

- Design them in advance, along a definite theme that ties in with your curriculum.

With a little imagination, you can take images that are available from a variety of sources and weave them into excellent bulletin board presentations. Pictures from old magazines, newspaper headlines, posters, photographs, construction paper, flannel boards and flannel, cartoons, comic strips, simple line drawings and a host of other items are available at little or no cost.

Make Banners and Streamers

Some of the most attractive banners I have seen have been made from discarded fabrics, carpet samples, newsprint paper or other materials which are readily available for little or no cost.

In fact, even if you have a large materials budget, it is better to use low-cost materials for most banners so that you can justify changing them frequently. Some youth leaders even change the banners every week. They say it helps them create a new mood to enhance the program theme, and they point out that it can create a whole new environment every week.

Use Simple Puppets

Hand puppets can be made from paper sacks, socks, old clothes and many other items you can retrieve from the discard piles. Use your imagination. For example, take the tops from two Leggs-brand pantyhose containers, glue a large button on each, and you've got a great set of bugeyes for a "Cookie Monster" type of character. That's how the people on "Sesame Street" got their first model. Look for imaginative ways to use sections of egg cartons, jar lids, balloons, ping pong balls, milk jugs — anything that can double for eyes, a mouth, arms, legs or a head. You can have a lot of fun making puppets, and use them effectively to present messages.

Add Audio for Greater Impact

When you add an audio track to your visual presentations, you can substantially increase the impact. Media specialists speak of the "synergistic effect" of mixing sound with visual images. It basically means that, when sight and sound are combined, they produce a greater impact than the total of the two if used separately.

Again, audiovisuals don't have to be complicated or expensive. For example, have someone take a lot of slides of a retreat. Select slides that give a complete pictoral history of a trip — from the time you left the church until you returned. Capture all the moods and as much of the program content as possible. Now, add a song like Willie Nelson's "On the Road Again," and change the slides to the rhythm of the music. You've got a dynamite show that will reinforce the things you tried to convey on the retreat. And if I were a gambler, I'd bet your young people will ask to see it several times. If you want to get a little more elaborate with it, mix together parts from several songs to change the mood to fit the slides and show the various feelings the young people experienced on the trip.

Here's another cheap idea for an effective program-launcher. Many people now have videocassette recorders. Tape a short segment from a newscast or dramatic show and bring it to the meeting. Play the segment and use it as a discussion-starter, or to reinforce a point you are trying to get across.

This section is not designed to provide an exhaustive list of audiovisual ideas. It is only to stimulate your thinking about some of the possibilities that are readily available to you for making your program come alive.

Get the Young People Involved

If you've ever been to a concert by an amateur band, you know how comfortable teenagers are in working with media. It's their ballgame!

When you get them involved in putting together various media to communicate with other young people, they will demonstrate an amazing enthusiasm for what you are doing. They will also surprise you with their ability to come up with resources for getting things done. Someone will bring a cassette player, someone else will bring a turntable, and a mixer, and a slide projector, and an amplifier, etc. Pretty soon you'll have a studio that has remarkable capabilities.

Now, some of the sights and sounds they will come up with will be pretty bad — especially at the beginning. But that's OK! They will learn that they can make a valuable contribution to the group, that they can work together, and they will get excited about what they are doing.

Of course, you will have to guide the projects pretty carefully. They can get terribly gimmicky, and might go off on tangents which may be distracting rather than adding to what you are doing. But remember, it is easier to control excited youngsters than it is to resurrect a bunch of corpses.

A few examples of the kinds of things they could put together are:

- soundtracks for puppet shows
- soundtracks for slide presentations
- mock television or radio commercials for upcoming events
- man-on-the-street interviews for discussion-sparkers
- musical programs for banquets or other special occasions
- bulletin boards and banners
- collages
- making puppets

The electronic revolution that has taken place during the last decade has created a tremendous opportunity for churches to communicate more effectively with their youth, and to reach out to other young people in the community. Unfortunately, many youth leaders are sleeping right through it.

Enable Youth to Connect the Bible with Real Life

If the gospel of Christ has any vitality to it, it stems from the fact that Jesus entered the arena of human activity and longs to have an impact on every facet of each individual's daily life.

Your task as a youth leader is to help young people connect what is said in the Scriptures with what takes place every day of their lives. The measure of your success is not so much what takes place in their lives at 7 p.m. Sunday (or whenever your group meets) but what happens at 11 a.m. on Thursday, or 8 p.m. on Saturday.

Enabling youth to connect the Bible with real life involves much more than getting them to say "religious things" during planned functions. It includes enabling them to discover the dynamic character of the Gospel, which can penetrate redemptively into every area of their lives.

The Bible Speaks to Personal Concerns

Every major psychological study done in the last two decades has pointed to the fact that self-image is the greatest single factor in determining how successful and happy a person will be. People who grow up with a strong sense of personal identity and high self-esteem find that they have the inner resources to cope with the hard knocks of life, while people with low self-esteem tend to feel defeated, alone and unlovable.

Likewise, people who have self-confidence tend to view life positively, to be hopeful about themselves, and to be courageous in offering their contributions to the world.

Again and again, the Bible assures us that we are deemed lovable by the very sovereign of the universe. It encourages us to accept ourselves as wonderful creations of a loving God. It wipes away loneliness through assurances that God will always be with us in the struggles of life, and by its strong emphasis on Christian fellowship and mutual support among Christians.

Creative youth programming seeks to help young people forge a strong positive self-image, self-confidence and a definite personal identity through applying the Gospel to the daily experiences of life.

The Bible Speaks to Family Relationships

The adolescent years are often very stormy, and family relationships tend to break down at a time when the young person needs them most. Young people are often caught between their need for independence and personal identity and their need for the caring, supportive relationships of a strong family life. Creative programming enables young people to understand the family from God's perspective, and seeks to strengthen family connections.

The Bible Speaks to Connections with the World

Today's young people are concerned about their peers, their communities, and the world in which they live. Many live in fear of nuclear destruction, of rampant pollution of the environment, and worldwide depression.

The Bible not only speaks with hope about the ultimate destiny of mankind, it offers guidelines for personal relationships and response to the needs and dangers of a world filled with great challenges.

Creative youth programming helps young people sort out their concerns for and responsibilities toward all people and institutions with which they are connected.

Master Small-Group Techniques

The backbone of any youth ministry is the small group. In fact, the strongest benefit the church has to offer young people in an alienated world is the opportunity to make significant contact with other young people through small groups.

Yet many youth directors feel reluctant to lead small group discussions and activities for several reasons:

- They have difficulty getting good discussions going because they don't know what questions to ask.

- They fear the group will go off on tangents and not stick to the subject.

- They fear that someone will ask a question for which they have no answer.

- They fear that one young person will hurt the feelings of others in the group.

- They feel guilty about allowing young people to talk to each other without having something positive to contribute to the discussion.

- They prefer to give out information, rather than to allow young people to search through questions and issues.

- The fear that one or two people will dominate the discussions, and that timid individuals will feel left out.

Pointers for Small Group Discussions

1. *Always lead off with strong input.* Small groups react more easily to situations posed through questions, skits, cassettes or other methods of setting the pace. Once a direction is set and interest brought to a keen edge, people will participate readily and be easier to keep on track.

2. *Use questions to pull the group back on track if the discussion begins to wander.* A mind-bending

question can usually capture a wayward group. If questions don't pull the group back, you might try a comment like, "This is interesting. Perhaps we can talk about this next week, but right now I think there are some in the group who want to explore the main topic."

3. ***Don't feel that you have to have all the answers.*** Some of the most effective group leaders are those who are willing to admit they don't know everything. Be willing to say, "I don't know." There are some possible follow-ups that you can add. Here are a few: "I'll find out and report back to you," or "Let's talk about it some to see if someone in the group can give us some insight," or "Let's invite a specialist in the field to visit our group and talk about it."

4. ***Lay down some simple guidelines for the group, and carefully enforce them.*** Some things you might consider are: 1. No physical abuse; 2. No personal attacks on an individual; 3. Stick to the subject at hand. If you feel someone is being hurt by the comments of another, call the offending person into line and seek to reassure the injured person.

5. ***Don't be afraid to allow the discussion to roll along without input from you — providing it is following a positive vein.*** Young people will learn from each other better than they will from an adult. In fact, your primary goal for groups is to get the members to talk among themselves. As long as they are on track, learning and enjoying the discussion, sit back and watch it work.

6. ***Seek to enable participants to discover truths for themselves rather than giving out too much information.*** When you tell young people a truth, it is yours, but when they discover it themselves, it is theirs.

7. ***Make sure everyone participates.*** You can usually control the "motor mouth" by directing the discussion to others through questions. And you can usually get timid people to talk by asking them direct questions that call for more than a yes or no answer. If the problem persists, you might set up a rule that calls for a comment from everyone in the group before a person speaks twice on a subject. Certainly every

discussion should be started by allowing each person to make a comment.

8. ***Make silence work for you.*** Some leaders panic when a group is silent for more than a few seconds. They will jump in to try to ease the tension. Often, when we do that, we interrupt a person who was about to break the silence. When you ask a good strong question, and the group sits silently, wait until someone responds, or ask a particular person to comment. Some of the greatest discussions are started by long periods of reflective silence. Don't be afraid of it!

9. ***Stay in touch with the feelings and needs of the group you would lead.*** The greatest tools for leading a group discussion are not your mouth and your hands, but your ears. Good group leaders are masters at listening to what the members of the group are saying.

10. ***Feed back to group members what you are hearing them say.*** Focus for them the underlying implications of the attitudes and ideas they are expressing. It helps them to think through the subject and their positions on it.

Conclusion

In this chapter, I have focused on creative approaches to programming for young people. We have talked primarily about methods and techniques.

A caution is in order: *The youth in your group are people — methods are only vehicles for helping them grow.* Youth ministry becomes gimmicky when methods matter more than people. Any effort to be creative in programming must have as its primary goal to move the young people toward greater personal and spiritual maturity. Otherwise, it is a waste of time, resources and golden opportunities.

GROWTH EXERCISE

As you review each section of this chapter, set a goal for using the principles of the section more effectively in your youth ministry. The questions below might help you focus those goals:

1. *Since young minds are usually the greatest source of creativity, how will you use more advantageously the creativity of your group?*

2. *Is your meeting place a learning/growth center? Does it have a purpose and plan? Does it have adequate resource people? Does it have adequate resource materials?*

3. *How effectively do you use media in communicating with your group? Do you take full advantage of visuals? of audiovisuals? Are your young people involved in the preparation and use of media?*

4. *Does your youth program help young people to connect the Bible with the real world in which they live? Does it help them apply the principles of the Gospel to their personal concerns? family relationships? relationships with the world?*

5. *How effectively do you lead small group discussions?*

CHAPTER 13

A Positive Approach to Evaluation

*A young seminary graduate was invited to preach his first sermon,
in his home church. Excitedly, he prepared for weeks, practiced and
nervously paced the floor.*

*Finally, he decided to write it out and read it — so he wouldn't
leave out a single gem he had prepared for the "home folks."*

*At the close of the service, he was standing at the door receiving
the compliments of his friends and family. Suddenly, he was face to
face with his grandmother, who always told it like it was!*

*"Well, Granny," he asked, beaming, "how'd I do on my first
sermon?"*

"I only saw three things wrong," the old lady replied.

*"Only three mistakes in my first sermon? Not bad!" Then he
asked the wrong question: "What were they?"*

*"First," said the old lady, "you read it! Secondly, you read it
poorly! And thirdly, it wasn't worth reading anyway!"*

Not many of us can take that kind of evaluation! Fortunately,
few of us will ever have to take it.

Yet some youth leaders avoid evaluation as if they feel their
egos are on the line with every question they ask. They interpret all
criticism as a personal attack, all suggestions for improvement as
rejections of their ideas, and all compliments as proof of their abilities.

That attitude has little to do with what I mean by *evaluation*.

What Is Evaluation?

Evaluation is an organized system for determining how effectively you have done what you set out to do, and discovering ways of
doing it better in the future.

It involves gathering information, asking opinions and pro-
cessing what you learn to improve your performance. Evaluation

gives you an orderly approach to learning from your mistakes, failures and successes.

The Role of Criticism in Evaluation

Whether or not you ask for opinions, some people will give them. It's called criticism, and there are two kinds of criticism: constructive and petty. I suggest that you simply learn to ignore petty criticism, which comes from chronic grumblers. Some people will never be pleased!

But constructive criticism can be a valuable aid in evaluation. It can give you an entirely different perspective from which you can gain insights. Value the person who cares enough to point out mistakes you might not have noticed, to offer suggestions for better ways of doing things, and to help you determine the relative effectiveness of your methods.

Tools of Evaluation

Carefully chosen questions are your primary tools for evaluating. They fall into two categories: questions you ask others to gain objective input, and questions you ask of yourself to help you organize your appraisal. To be of real value, those questions should be very pointed, easy to answer, and designed to produce specific information.

For example, if you are evaluating a banquet speaker, it might not help you much to ask, "Did you like (not like) the speaker?" — especially if he is the pastor's brother-in-law. It might be more helpful to ask a select group to evaluate him on a scale of 1 to 10 on each of the following points: timeliness of topic, preparation, presentation, audience involvement and audience response.

When to Evaluate?

It is a good idea to evaluate everything you do, as soon as is practical, after you have done it. This suggests constant and ongoing evaluation.

Young people and volunteers tend to answer questions based on their feelings at the moment those questions are asked. For example, if you wait a week after a retreat to ask young people how they felt about the retreat, their answers might reflect more what has happened in their lives during the intervening week than what took place on the retreat.

How to Evaluate?

Questions should be developed — before an event — to give you insights into each of the following areas:

- How close were your goals and objectives to the needs and desires of the group?

- How near did you come to reaching your goals?

- How effective were the strategies you used? (Evaluate each strategy separately.)

- Did you miss any opportunities?

- What strategies should be tried again?

- Are there any ideas for new techniques and methods?

It is helpful to evalute everything. For example, after a retreat you should evaluate: food, transportation, recreation, program content and methods, resource people, speakers, costs and accommodations.

It is always a good idea to put a synopsis of your evaluation into a file for reference in future planning and in setting next year's goals.

A Backward Look at the Book

Most youth leaders I know work very hard at helping young people to grow spiritually and personally. In fact, many of them work too hard at it.

The key to effectiveness is not to be found in *how much you do,* but rather in *what you do.* I have tried to share with you ideas that have worked for me and for countless other youth leaders.

I believe the most helpful thing you can glean from the entire book is: *Losers concentrate on activities; winners concentrate on their goals.* If you would be an effective youth leader, learn to develop goals that will produce the results you desire; develop plans that will help you reach those goals; and work the plans you have developed. It is the only way to take maximum advantage of the talents and opportunities God has given all of us.

May your life be as richly rewarded by serving young people as has mine!

If You Enjoyed
*What Works & What Doesn't
in Youth Ministry,*
You'll Get All The How-To's From
These Other Meriwether Publishing
Youth Ministry Books:

YOUTH MINISTRY FROM START TO FINISH
by JANET LITHERLAND

IT'S SUNDAY NIGHT AGAIN?
by DONNA GLADMAN

What Works & What Doesn't in Youth Ministry provided you inspiration for reviving or starting up a youth ministry in your church. And it took you into teens' minds, so you can build a ministry that will ring true to them. But now you'd like some specific ideas. What are the kinds of goals you'd like to set? How do you work with church boards to get the resources you need? How do you organize complex youth activities without getting bogged down? What kinds of things *do* teens like to do? And how can you make the Bible relevant to their up-to-the-minute lives? You'll find all the procedures, work charts, surveys, retreat ideas, craft programs and fund-raising information you need in *Youth Ministry from Start to Finish,* by best-selling author Janet Litherland, and in *It's Sunday Night Again?,* by Donna Gladman. These books are required reading for anyone who thinks nurturing the spiritual lives of youth is important. Both paperback books are available at bookstores or from Meriwether Publishing Ltd., P.O. Box 7710, Colorado Springs, Colorado 80933.

4261-2
5-05